Miniature Mania
140 and counting!

Sue Passmore

All rights reserved
Copyright © Sue Passmore, 2020

Sue Passmore is hereby identified as the author of this work in accordance with section 77 of the copyright, designs and patents act 1988.

ISBN 978-1-71672-606-4

Dedicated to

Marion Osborne, *Triang* guru;
Celia Thomas of *Ktminiatures*,
and Lin Hodder of *JLB*
who organised the trips to dollshouse fairs

Introduction

Like most little girls of my generation I had a dollshouse which I played with endlessly. Mine was made for me by Great-Uncle Taylor, a former sea-captain, when I was three years old and was very nearly big enough for me to get into at that age. But I never thought that one day I would have over 140 miniature houses and roomboxes. In fact I only came into the hobby in the late 1990s when I was retired; my arthritis made research difficult and I had temporarily to give up writing academic articles. What I had not realised was that in the meantime interest in dollshouses, collecting historic ones and creating them oneself had gained world-wide popularity and I was simply bowled over. I made these discoveries when a new dollshouse shop was opened at Tywyn, Merioneth, in 1998, by Eve who had formerly run Serenity Manors in Lichfield. It was an eye-opener! Cramfull of every kind of miniaturised object you could think of. Here I was introduced to the popular magazines catering for the hobby: *Dollshouse & Miniature Scene*, *Dollshouse World* and *International Dollshouse News*, and later to *The Dollshouse Magazine*. These too were inspirational. I began modestly enough, by buying some minute horse brasses though had nowhere as yet to put them. However, I still retained a few dollshouse items from the original house, kept for sentimental reasons, like the sofa and armchair made by my Aunt Mavis's husband, Leslie Ridout, in the 1940s, from an old leather driving coat and a grandfather clock incorporating an old watch. I was also inspired by an article in *Dollshouse & Miniature Scene* November 1998, which showed how to make a "metal" bed and patchwork quilt, done in felt pen. I had a Victorian china headed doll found in an oddments tray in an antique shop, still in her original clothes, apart from a lace tippet I added, and new feet as her china feet had long ago been broken off. These were modelled in Fimo, an air dried clay which could also be hardened in a cool oven, and this was to become an invaluable material for making many things. So I began making a two room house in an orangebox, like so many wartime children did, though the orangebox was becoming an endangered species by then and I was lucky to find one at a local supermarket. The sittingroom also houses a German metal tray, one of my childhood toys, but which probably belonged to my Aunt Sue, born in 1898, and a 1940s Toby Jug made by Barton, one of the major makers of dollshouse furniture in the twentieth century in Britain whose history has been documented by Mrs Marion Osborne in one of her invaluable sourcebooks for this era: *Barton's Model Homes, A History of A Barton & Co's (Toys) Ltd 1945-1984*, available from Mrs Marion Osborne, 29 Attingham Lane, Chilwell, Nottingham, NJ9 5JP. I called it Brick House because of its brick paper facade. It is really rather crudely made and I should certainly do things differently now, but it has a certain charm and I have retained it as it was, adding appropriate china items and another antique child doll, visiting her grandmother. The pipecleaner black cat is an old friend, my mascot when taking my O level exams! The fireplace is a modern resin one with a brass fender got at an antique shop. The dressingtable is a cheap slot together piece then commonly available in toyshops, but carefully painted and a real mirror added; the china hip bath was acquired at Tywyn, and I made the old fashioned clothes airer.

Brick House, sitting room.

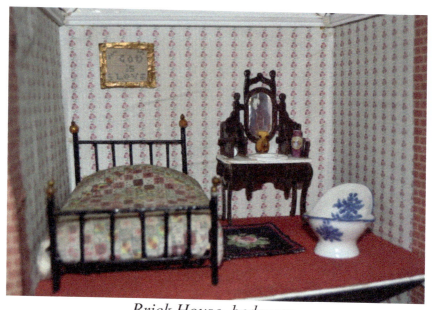

Brick House, bedroom.

Some of the exquisite little items on the mantlepiece were either gifts from the magazines I now took or acquired at dollshouse fairs, another delightful discovery, especially Miniatura held at the NEC in Birmingham, twice a year. I embroidered the small mats too, in fact one of the most attractive things about the hobby to me was the scope for needlework of all kinds, and my beds were always properly fitted out from the mattress up. Most magazines carried embroidery patterns and one could also buy books on the subject of miniature embroidery. The hobby also appealed to me in other creative ways, I come from a family with several artists, and I can't even draw. But the dollshouses made me feel creative as I learnt to make 3D scenes, paint backgrounds and even to fake mahogany! The research required to produce a historically accurate scene was also appealing. A lot of inspiration has come from paintings and from books.

There follows a list of items from the collection displayed in the book, begining with themed items, in historical order, followed by Collectibles and Very Small Scale. Not the entire collection by any means but just over half.

Themed Items:

Quentin Matsys, Tudor for a Tenner, 16th century, *13*
Stromer House 17th century, *18*
Van Amstel, early 18th cent paper House, *25*
Gabriel Metsu: The Cello Player, De Stolp House 17th Century, *27*
Gustavian Room 18th century, *30*
Flemish beguinage, *31*
Plas Melyn 18th century, *33*
Ladies of Llangollen Tower late 18th century, *40*
Regency House early 19th century, *45*
The Wightman House, 19th century, *51*
Thomas & Jane Welsh Carlyle House 1857, *53*
Elizabeth Barrett Browning Salon in 1860, *58*

Burges Gatehouse late 19th century, *60*
Victorian Shadowbox, *64*
Sagamore Hill 1890s, *66*
Dunham Coconut House 1890s, *70*
Mittel Europa Interior about 1900, *75*
Charles Rennie Mackintosh house, *79*
Demel's Bakery & Café, *87*
Place Du Tertre, *92*
Shell Villa, *95*
Ginger & Pickles Shop, *98*
Charleston, *102*
Teapot Dome: The Roaring Twenties, *106*
Steamship Office, *109*
Art Deco Interior: Mavis Bank, *112*
Little Grey Rabbit House, *116*
Larsson house, *119*
Corfu Villa - My Family and Other Animals, *123*
World War II house, *128*
Kiosk, *135*
Railway Waiting Room, *136*
1960s House, *139*
Fenton Tower, *148*
Cairngorm Castle, *152*
Sue's Toy Shop, *161*
Dress Shop, *166*
Cleddau Crafts, *170*
Antiques Shop Interior, *176*

The Mount: a transformation, *183*
Smugglers' Inn, *188*
Seaside Shop & beachscene, *192*
Backstage, *195*
Garden, *198*
Church, *200*
Easter Roombox, *204*
Christmas Scene & House, *206*

Collectibles:

Das Biedermeier Spielzeughaus, *212*
Marks & Spencer Paper Shop, *214*
German tin bathroom, *216*
Gottschalk House, *218*
Wagner House, *221*
Yellow House furniture, *224*
Princess Elizabeth's Welsh Cottage by Triang, *228*
Stone Court: a Hobbies House, 1932, *233*
1930s Bungalow, *238*
Dwarfs' Cottage, *240*
Dutch Warehouse, *242*
Tin houses, American and one Chad Valley, 245
Amersham House, *259*
Henllan, *262*
Group of Triangs & Sherborne, *265*
Group of GeeBees, *287*

Sylvanian Windmill, *302*
Sylvanian Canal Boat, *306*
Petite Properties' Cowslip Cottage, *308*
MOMA, *312*

<u>Very Small Scale:</u>

Bicentennial Betsy Ross House, *313*
Malamute Saloon, *316*
WWI Hospital, *318*
CRM Tearoom, *320*
A Park, *322*
Dollshouse' Dollshouse, *323*

<u>A restoration project:</u>
Cardigan Castle Dollshouse, *325*

TUDOR FOR A TENNER

After making Brick House I was hooked, and my next attempt was "Tudor for a Tenner", inspired by a series of excellent articles in back numbers of *Dollshouse & Miniature Scene* between April and October 1997. I built it between November and April 1998-1999. One was shown how to make a room at a time, very solidly constructed from the covers of wallpaper books which I begged from a local DIY shop; and other items made from cereal boxes like the roof tiles and the doors made from several layers of cardboard. Friends obliged with their empty cereal packets. And Whiskas dried food boxes supplied three of the hearths. It was a painstaking task, rooms panelled slowly by hand, whereas nowadays you can buy sheets of panelling. But it was great fun and meticulous care was taken in reproducing the great hearth in the kitchen and a spit that actually turned. And while making it I established a principle which was to influence many of my creations, they should have a specific theme. In this instance my son Guy suggested that I should base one room on the countinghouse depicted in the painting by Quentin Matsys, a Flemish painter, who in 1512 painted a detailed picture of the 'Moneylender and his wife', a copy of which hangs on the wall of that room, and I endeavoured to recreate everything that appeared in the painting. Much of the furniture is home-made, though there is a Barton's "tudor" chair in the bedroom. The settle in the kitchen opens up to show the servant's bedding as he sleeps there. The authentic copy of a Tudor food cupboard with its pierced door to allow air to circulate, came from the fascinating dollshouse shop in the Parade at Shrewsbury and cost as much as to make the house itself! The servant, Roger, is by Playmobil, dressed according to a pattern in the *DHMS* series. The chest in the countinghouse contains small bags of cash (sequins), and I have added the crossbow as it is a Flemish hobby shooting at bunches of feathers on a tall pole. It has been great fun adding appropriate items like the majolica plate and red glass on the sideboard upstairs as no house is ever entirely "finished", you can go on adding things to your heart's content. I made the leather screen alongside, from one seen in the magazine *World of Interiors*. And also the illuminated book on the settle, from a plastic scrap picked up on the road by a friend who, like me, values "found objects". Though there is a beautifully made facsimile of the Lord's Prayer in the book on the table in front of the Moneylender's wife, there are so many makers of exquisite items to be found at Miniatura, like the beautiful little chess table with its magnetic chess set so you can actually play a game. It is genuine sheep's wool in the basket by the spinning wheel in the main bedroom, collected by me from hedgerows and washed. The four poster made by me has a truckle bed beneath it and the baby's cradle alongside. I like the baby walker too, a copy of a contemporary one, and the Noah's Ark. The enamel shields which adorn the Whiskas hearths show the various provinces of Belgium and were taken from a bracelet bought there when I was young.

Tudor for a Tenner

The Moneylender and wife, based on a painting by Quentin Matsy

A SEVENTEENTH CENTURY HOUSE

Collecting miniature objects and providing them with an appropriate setting is a very old hobby, and some superb houses survive from the 17th and 18th century in the Netherlands and Germany and the Victoria & Albert Museum of Childhood at Bethnal Green has one too. These houses are valuable historical documents as they are furnished in such detail with contemporary artefacts, they are a real peepshow into the past. Absolutely no expense was spared by the wealthy merchants' wives who owned them, often items were made in real silver, and there were exquisite examples of porcelain and glass in miniature. Lin Hodder of JLB, a dollshouse supplier, whom I met at Miniatura, organised regular visits to Soest Dollshouse Fair in Germany and one year included a visit to Nuremberg where some of the finest old houses are to be found. I longed to make a copy of a house dated from 1639, known as the Stromer house, as the original owner was a Baron von Stromer. As it happened, my niece gave me a large wooden winebox and I saw at once how it might be extended to give stabling beneath as in the original house and filled in to provide several rooms. It is not intended as an exact facsimile but to convey the style of these early houses. In fact the courtyard on the right is copied from the Strasbourg house of 1680 with its well, bee skeps and chickens. All these houses are illustrated in Leonie Wilckens' magnificent book *Mansions in Miniature*, but for reproducing much of the detail I relied on the coloured illustrations in Faith Eaton's *The Ultimate Dollshouse Book*. I am particularly pleased with the painted exteriors, the windows and stable boy in the doorway are exact copies from the originals. I have even copied the elaborately decorated ceilings though impossible to see unless the house is upended. The doll inhabitants are all antique, the porcelain doll with moulded plaits came from Ilona Stahl's stall at Soest Dollshouse Fair as did the blond china head of the cook for whom I made a body; the smallest doll was bought from Ktminiatures. All are dressed by me in clothes appropriate to the 17th century. The furniture is wooden German furniture and mostly dates from the early part of the twentieth century, acquired at Miniatura from S W Golland's excellent stall of second hand furniture but goes well with the house. The chairs with blue paper trim were bought at Ktminiatures and date from about 1910. The swan sleigh stored above the stable was made from a kit bought at Soest. The dresser in the kitchen is modern but made by Sandy Eismont (bought at Miniatura) in the style of Nuremberg dressers with a chicken coop below. The doors even have tiny working snibs. On it are some early twentieth century wooden German bowls and jug, as well as "pewter" plates, actually tin, but painted with silver paint to look older, and a tiny working hour glass found at Miniatura. The old tin stove with its oversize Britannia pots, was bought on the Golland's stall. I built up the chimney breast and arranged the modern metal plates as in the original house. The German bed was extended to make a fourposter and it even has a scene painted inside the tester. As Leonie Wickens advises, regarding the bedding popular at the time, the lower mattress is literally a strawsack, with a shallower wool stuffed one above it, the blanket and pillow came with the bed.

As a tribute to my mother I used an old silk scarf of hers to drape the bed. The cow was hard to find but a well-modelled one the right size turned up at Miniatura. The horse is actually a plastic zebra painted white and given a mane and tail. One of the most enchanting things in the house is a tiny jointed metal doll made to resemble the wooden Dutch dolls so popular once as children's playthings, and that was acquired at a lovely dollshouse shop in Penarth, near Cardiff.

Stromer house, kitchen

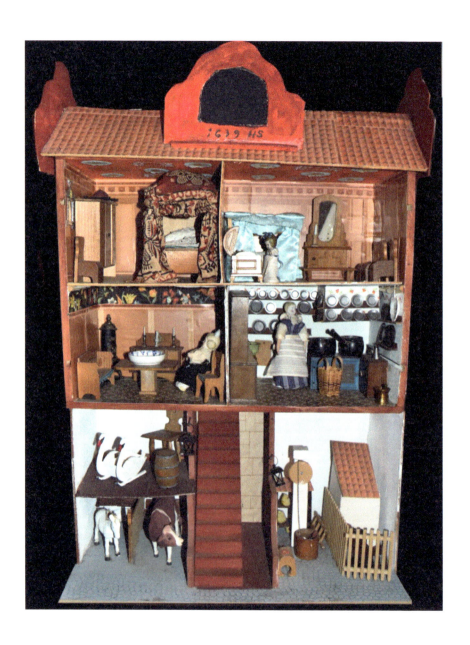

Stromer house, basement

SARA PLOOST VAN AMSTEL HOUSE IN HAARLEM

I have managed to see all the great Dutch houses, and at the Franz Hals museum in Haarlem bought a paper kit to make a facsimile of Sarah Ploost van Amstel's house which shows the fabulous setting this merchant's wife created for her tiny treasures. Sara lived from 1699 to 1751.

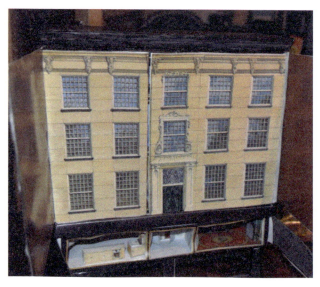

ANOTHER 17TH CENTURY INTERIOR

This was created in a charming kit house made by De Stolp. Its exterior shape reminded me instantly of an enchanting book we had as children: *The Adventures of Kwik and Kwak*, who were two little Dutch ducks, so I painted the exterior to look like their house in Volendam.

However the inspiration for the downstairs room comes from the *Golden Age of Dutch Art*, the interiors of the artist Pieter de Hooch and the main figure is The Cello player by Gabriel Metsu, painted in 1658. Upstairs furnishings were inspired by Faith Eaton's detailed illustration from a cupboard house of the late 17th century. I made the Cello Player myself in order to ensure he was a faithful copy, his orange accoutrements were cut from one of the children's outgrown anoraks! The other two dolls heads were found on a Berlin bombsite. These little china heads must be incredibly tough, they are often all that survive of the original dolls and in Orkney I saw a china head in the window of the harbour master's office, which had come ashore from a shipwreck.

The panelling came from a Hattonwoods catalogue. The foot warmer lined with metal is typical of the period. The sleigh on the right is Dutch, but bought like the De Stolp kit at Miniatura. The small object like a lidded frying pan upstairs is similar to early Dutch bedwarmers. The overhead drying rack is seen in the laundry room of many Dutch houses as are wicker basket trays in which clothes were carried (not shown).

Gabriel Metsu, 'The Cello Player'

AN 18th CENTURY GUSTAVIAN ROOM

Over the years I have made innumerable roomboxes to various themes, but this was one of the first. I have always been a fan of the simple Swedish 18th century style named for their then ruler, and seen full size rooms in Swedish museums furnished in this way. The inspiration came from a set of cutout panels offered by a dollshouse magazine and also from Jessica Ridley's *The Decorated Dollshouse*. I made the stove and the grey painted table is typical as is the use of check material, what we call gingham. I made the willow pattern screen (that design became hugely popular in the 18th century) from a Les Chats pattern, they were regular exhibitors at Miniatura, and I dressed the peg doll.

A FLEMISH BEGUINAGE

The idea of a beguinage - a place where pious women could live retired lives without taking monastic vows grew up in the 13th century and you will find several such little colonies in Belgian and Dutch towns, one of the best known is at Bruges. The women lived in separate cottages but worshipped together at a church on the site, they are often built round a little green. I came across this typically Flemish-style kit at Arnhem Miniatures Fair on a trip arranged by JLB. The only instructions were available in Dutch and cost an extra 9 euros on top of the 9 for the kit.

It proved rather fiddly to make, each window required cutting 12 separate pieces of wood. It is furnished very simply as a single room but with very good quality furniture, bed, chair, table and stove, as the women were not poor. The doll, a kit got at Arnhem also, was dressed following a pattern in the *Dollshouse Magazine* of April 2004. The lace pillow was discovered at the Georgian House, a dollshouse shop in Cardigan. As lacemaking is a well-known activity in Bruges, I was delighted to include that. The crosses I already owned but the effigy of the Virgin Mary was made at the monastery on Caldy Island and bought at the monks' shop in Tenby.

Beguinage

PLAS MELYN: A GEORGIAN INTERIOR

This Riviera kit house was bought at the Old Barn, Aberaeron. It is made by Artemesia Latina, Barcelona. Its classical style made it suitable for the Georgian dollshouse I wished to create. I changed the original door and altered the window battens and made shutters for shutting over the windows inside at night. Of course real Georgian style kits were available but they were much dearer. I was greatly assisted by Brian Long's book: *The Authentic Georgian Dollshouse.*

I spent a long time looking at the colours of the houses in Aberaeron, being a town popularly said to have been designed by Beau Nash, to decide on the right colour for the exterior. The name Plas Melyn (Welsh for yellow, and Plas means a gentry house) was chosen because I envisaged the house as a tribute to the 18th century diarist Elizabeth Baker, whose diary extracts and letters I had edited for numerous articles in the Merioneth Historical and Record Society Journal and who was entertained at Plas Uchaf and Plas Coch in Dolgellau. She was poor for much of her later life but had she struck it rich with her mining ventures, I imagined this as the sort of house she might have lived in. Elizabeth noticed interior decoration and always praised houses to her taste. She is represented by the lady in a striped dress, the doll and dress bought at The Toy Cave, Aberystwyth, the cap - de rigeur at the time - made by me, entertaining friends in the upstairs drawingroom.

This Print Room was inspired by Jessica Ridley's in *The Decorated Dollshouse*, and the paper was acquired at Miniatura. All the colours and wallpapers used in the house are very much of the period as is the fairly minimalist formal arrangement of the downstairs reception room. The somewhat overdressed but not untypical Georgian ladies in the drawingroom were bought at the Georgian Dollshouse Shop in Cardigan and the perfectly attired wax gentleman came from there too. The Chinese lacquered tallboy in the drawingroom is probably the single most expensive piece of furniture I ever bought at £35, made by Golland's (Miniatura) who specialised in lacquer furniture as well as second hand pieces. The drawers are full of pressed flowers - a popular hobby in the 18th century. But the matching chest cost only £4 from Carmarthen Market. For a very short time nice home-made furniture was available at a stall there, made locally, but this perhaps was made in China, Margaret Towner in her *Dolls House Furniture a guide for collectors*, showed examples which were imported in the 1980s. The backgammon table is a modern travelling game with magnetised pieces, I made legs for it, knowing how popular "tables", as it was known then, was at the time. The corner fireplace is typical of the period and found in genuine old babyhouses as they were called in England in the 18th century. Most of the furniture is nicely made reproduction Georgian furniture but I covered the chairs more appropriately in striped silk. The very best materials I could find were used for curtains. I had intended to make the date of the house a little earlier than 1780 but discovered that curtain rings only came from France in that year, before that they were simply nailed up and tied back! The pineapple finial on the banisters came from a cocktail stick and I made the gilt mirror from Fimo and the candle sconces from scraps of gilt filigree found at a car boot sale. The grandfather clock was a cheap brass ornament originally supporting a thermometer, I painted it brown and provided a glass for the face from a disintegrated locket. The bedroom's Chinese wallpaper was photocopied from a postcard got at the Hague and the washbasin with its pail beneath was bought in Delft on the same jaunt. I made the bed from a Mini Mundus kit, and a beautifully made chair with a seat embroidered by Felicity Price at Miniatura is in the corner. The delicately embroidered silk shawl hanging on the door was made by Margaret of Miss Margaret's Hats who always appeared at Miniatura with a large jewelled spider brooch on her shoulder. The curtains in the bedroom are made from a handpainted silk scarf found in a charity shop. I took great pains with the kitchen too, helped by Brian Long's book, and made the grate, jack and spits to resemble actual 18th century items, also the water tank above the sink. The bread oven to the left of the hearth actually opens and propped against the fine settle which came from Hattonwoods is a wooden peel used for removing bread from the oven. Hattonwoods also provided the 3D flagstoned floor paper. The Dutch Oven was beautifully made by Sussex Crafts. Overhead hangs a bread car often seen in country places, to keep the bread away from mice. The numerous china and copper items came from Miniatura as did the dolly for washing clothes but the copper washing tub was found in a charity shop. Betty the maid, was the name of Elizabeth's actual maid, but I have also given her a peg doll cook who is making butter with tiny "butter hands", although in fact Elizabeth was a very good cook herself, and made wonderful meals from offal like cow-heels, from which she created Mock Turtle Soup. I have since edited and published her diary and, having grown fond of Elizabeth through all her trials, am pleased to have created a more elegant setting for her than her actual lodging for many years in a room rented from an excise officer, which Betty papered with newspaper as the walls were in such poor condition!

Plas Melyn

LADIES OF LLANGOLLEN TOWER

In 2003, the Dolls' House Emporium mail-order firm ran a competition. They offered for the reasonable sum of £28 a wooden hexagonal tower kit with base, and prizes like one of their beautiful Dollshouse kits of one's choice, for the most unusually decorated kit - one sent in three photos, and there were some superb entries. The winner was one who made a semi ruin of her tower! It looked as if she had set it on fire. But it was very effective, as a home for the wizard Merlin. For a long time I could not think of any inspiration, but looking through *Gardenmania*, a book of really over the top antique designs for gardens, given me by my daughter, I came across a rustic tower dated 1758, whose design I copied for mine. I chose to set it in Plas Newydd's garden with a painted background of Dinas Bran mountain with its ruined castle, near Llangollen, the home of the celebrated Ladies of Llangollen, who shocked the 18th century when they, as spinsters, set up home together. I made them in their customary masculine style riding habits (from a pattern in *Dolls' House Magazine* in August 2002), and their faithful maid Mary, to appear in the tower. The rocky landscape and the arch (carved from polystyrene) and model of the font the Ladies acquired from nearby Valle Crucis Abbey, typical of the period's passion for the antique and picturesque, are inspired by their garden which also contained an ornamental dairy and rustic summerhouse. Ornamental dairies were hugely fashionable at this period and some wonderful examples survive, at Woburn Abbey for instance and everyone will have heard of Marie Antoinette's Le Petit Hameau.

The Ladies of Llangollen, Sarah Ponsonby on the left, Lady Eleanor Butler on the right and my re-creation.

They did not have a shell grotto but as that was also very popular in the 18th century, I made a shell-lined room upstairs and the ornamental dairy downstairs. The staircase proved to be a bit of a headache as there was so little space, circular staircases could be bought but they were extremely expensive, so I made one very simply from triangular treads fitted on to a bamboo skewer. I made a churn for the dairy, copying an 18th century print in my possession, I also made a yoke for Mary with buckets. A lot of attractive items for the dairy were discovered at Old Bethpage Village shop on Long Island, USA, like the milking stool and wooden bowls. A later addition was the porcelain cat (not shown) licking up some spilt milk! The Ladies were extremely fond of cats and a painting of their cats is shown at Plas Newydd, which is open to the public.

Making the shell grotto was a fiddle and cost me about £10 in shells as I did not have enough variety in ones collected off beaches over the years but luckily our local shell shop provided enough in the end. The shells are set in plaster, which dried incredibly quickly so one needs to have the patterns firmly fixed in one's mind before one starts work.

The attractive stone benches inside and out and the urn came from the Georgian House in Cardigan. I wasn't even commended! But had enjoyed the creation of another little world which I should probably not have thought of otherwise.

REGENCY HOUSE

This house was found at an OpenAir Market held near New Quay, Ceredigion. I towed it home - about a mile - on my set of luggage wheels, which caused some curious looks from passing cars. It cost £18. It was obviously home-made, perhaps a facade attached to a cupboard base. The interior had one long room upstairs and three small ones downstairs as it appears in the photographs. The shallow roof was originally covered in modern brick paper. The facade was painted as it is now. Some one had obviously been to a great deal of trouble to make the elaborate windows and arched door. I added the coigning which you can buy from any dollshouse supplier, and tiled the roof. What attracted me also and determined the Regency style of the interior, was the fact that the long upstairs room could accommodate my Myriorama, a copy of a landscape game printed in Leipzig about 1826 and acquired from Llun a Gair (Picture & Word) Art Shop in Aberaeron, some time before. However you arrange the 24 cards they make a coherent landscape scene. This resembled wallpaper fashionable in that era - see *The Authentic Georgian House* by Brian Long. I applied them over the original green wallpaper. I also inserted floor coverings. I have replaced the original paper in two of the downstairs rooms, that on the right remained as it fitted in with my scheme. I inserted the staircase and glazed the windows and made the ruched curtains modelled on those at Number 1, Royal Crescent in Bath. They actually work - with care! The willow-pattern theme in the lower left bedroom was inspired by paper from Hattonwoods and material from JLB. The furniture was made by me and modelled on a set of actual Regency furniture sold at Sotheby's, the style of the bed is known as a polonaise. I used a simple wire-work bed as the basis. The Chinese paper in the hall was found at a fair in Freeport, on Long Island, USA. The Chinese Chippendale bed in the right-hand bedroom was copied from one illustrated in Caroline Hamilton's *Decorative Dolls' Houses*. The basement I constructed from a kit got at the Model Shop at the Old Barn, Aberaeron. I only used part of it, other pieces went to make the basement in the Stromer House. I immensely enjoyed making the elaborate diningroom inspired by Jessica Ridley's version in her book *The Decorated Dollshouse*. I revamped a basic Taiwan table and chairs in Regency Chinese style. The bamboo sideboard was found at the Open Air market too. The house is so over the top anyway I had no compunction about using the Adam-style wallpaper in the kitchen, blue paper was popular then as it was thought to repel flies. A false wall, with a door in it, conceals the cook's bedroom. The elaborate stove came from the Dolls House Emporium. The dresser was bought at Tiny Treasures, Cecil Street, Carlyle, a nice little shop with a good stock of unusual items. The rest of the kitchen furniture came as a Plan Georgian set, bought by my son Guy at the famous David Morgan store in Cardiff, now closed, as a Christmas gift. It ought perhaps to be painted but I love it the way it is. The cook has a Victorian china head, found at Arnhem Dollshouse Fair and I modelled her body and dressed her. Cheap but well-made modern Regency-style furniture fills the upstairs drawingroom, with the exception of a valuable Chinese lacquer firescreen made by Janet Reyburn, who had a stall at Miniatura.

As a fan of Jane Austen I could not resist giving the house the name of Number 4, Sydney Place in Bath, where Jane Austen and her family stayed on one of their visits. The interior is of course far grander than any lodging house would have been, but Jane was accustomed to grand interiors when staying with her wealthy brother Edward and had visited Stoneleigh Abbey when her mother's cousin Thomas Leigh inherited it. The peg dolls dressed to represent Jane and her sister Cassandra had been made for a roombox of Jane's dressingroom as described by her niece Caroline Austen who often visited her in it at Chawton House, quoted in Elizabeth Jenkins' biography. This had to be dismantled as some of the furniture, the desk for example and piano, were used in the drawingroom. On the piano is a copy of a piece of music Jane herself wrote out by hand and the desk - made by me - contains scraps of paper with the first sentence of *Pride & Prejudice*! The tea equipage is a fantastic resin piece.

Interiors of the Regency House.

Regency House, upstairs sitting room with Myriorama decoration.

Regency House, dining room

Regency House, the kitchen

THE WIGHTMAN HOUSE

This was inspired by the early 19th century parlour in the Wightman House in Oyster Bay, Long Island. I made it in an appliance box, which I painstakingly covered with clapboard and added a shingled roof, typical of Oyster Bay's older houses.

At Old Bethpage Village shop on Long Island I acquired a wooden Dutch doll kit, and at a farmhouse there saw a quilt on a frame like that here. A few days later serendipitously I was able to buy the identical set-up in miniature at Freeport Dollshouse Fair. I have tried to keep the austere atmosphere of the original room, reproducing items which appear in it including a miniature picture made from feathers. The internal window is actually a modern resin ornament but so effective in this setting. The circular rug is hand-knitted. I later added another Dutch doll, English-made, by Eric Horne, to assist with the quilting.

Interior of the Wightman House

THOMAS & JANE WELSH CARLYLE HOUSE 1857

This house represents 24, Cheyne Row in Chelsea, where the Carlyles lived from 1834 until Thomas's death in 1881. I had the idea of reproducing this house for several years, having been inspired by the Robert Tait painting, executed in 1857, showing the famous writer and his wife in their drawingroom. It appears on the cover of Thea Holme's book *The Carlyles at Home*. But the problem was finding a suitable house.

A commissioned one would have cost £200. However, at the Georgian Dollshouse Shop in Cardigan I found a very solid kit house, similar to those made by Barbara's Mouldings, for £32. It was a tall five-roomed house with three window spaces and a door cut in it. The facade was unsuitable to represent the house, but looking at it laterally it would give the depth needed for the Carlyle House which was three rooms deep, each floor having a large closet behind the two main rooms on each floor. The effect of the closets would be achieved by tromp l'oeil doors, I had to omit the basement kitchen, and the staircases. I could provide the groundfloor drawingroom shown in the Tait painting, and the diningroom beyond it, the library and Jane's bedroom on the next floor; the third floor was not described in the guidebook to the house and in fact is not shown by the National Trust which owns the house which I visited, but made it into Thomas's writingroom under the eaves, as his was at the top of the house. The staff at the house were very interested in my project and helpful as I crawled about the floor looking at table-legs! I had to make a new facade and back for the house out of mountcard, and photocopied the picture of the real house for the former.

It was a challenge to find identical furniture and ornaments: the Camno Workshop, rather appropriately based in Scotland, provided chairs similar to those which Jane had inherited from her father Dr Welsh. I made the pictures and I had to embroider the carpet which runs through the groundfloor, which was a major task with its small repeat pattern. Jane liked fitted carpets even going so far as eking out insufficient ones with bits of dyed felt as they were not well-off.

I was fortunate enough to find suitable dolls at Miniatura Dolls' House Fair, resembling the portraits, and I dressed them myself. I was unable to find material appropriate to Thomas's dressing-gown, so put him in day clothes but otherwise everything else was as accurate as possible. Even his clay pipe turned up at Miniatura. Jane was a prolific letter writer, one of the best ever in that genre. In fact her writings have remained more popular than the historical works of her cranky husband, though he was famous enough in his day to be offered burial in Westminster Abbey. So I culled lots of details of her housekeeping from her letters. I had to make the sofa which appears in the painting and the curtains were copied from it too. Jane referred to chintz curtains in her bedroom and the red bed in which she had been born at Haddington in East Lothian, Scotland. It was a struggle to find an approriate dog for Jane's Nero who appears in the painting: "The only one satisfied with his portrait" as Jane remarked caustically! Chico the canary's cage appears in the diningroom, along with a scrap screen copying Jane's.

It was gratifying that the staff at 24 Cheyne Walk were so delighted with the photographs I sent them of the house, that they used the drawing room scene for their Christmas Card that year and even asked if I had re-created any other Trust houses in miniature.

The Carlyle house, interiors.

ELIZABETH BARRET BROWNING ROOMBOX 1860

Most people will know the romantic story of the poets Elizabeth Barret and Robert Browning who eloped to marry at St Marylebone church, as Elizabeth's tyrannical father would not consider marriage for any of his children and then settled in Italy where they lived happily ever after.

This roombox was suggested by the painting of the Brownings' salon in Florence by George Miginaty in 1861, shortly after Elizabeth died, commissioned by her husband Robert. I saw it in a collection of Elizabeth's letters to Mrs David Ogilvy, edited by Peter Haydon and Philip Kelley. The original is in the Gorwey Collection, Mills College Library. Photographs in the book also helped me model Robert and Elizabeth and their son Pen. A comparison will show how faithfully I have copied the room, though I could wish it had been possible to recreate it in something handsomer than a cardboard box! But it had to be large enough to accommodate the quantities of furniture, most of which I had to make or adapt. I am particularly proud of the frame over the fireplace which I modelled from Fimo and gilded. The invalid lounging chairs were also tricky to make, Elizabeth was frail lifelong. I faithfully hunted out suitable pictures and made most of the books. There are miniature copies of

Elizabeth's own letters in the desk. Even the ceiling design has been copied from the painting. It proved hardest to find Flush her spaniel, but eventually I acquired him at Britannia Miniatures who specialise in animals, by mail order.

Elizabeth Barret Browning roombox and, below, the painting that inspired it.

WILLIAM BURGES GATEHOUSE

I am a fan of the Victorian art-architect, as he described himself, William Burges, one of the most imaginative designers of the 19th century, having seen his work at Cardiff Castle, Castell Coch and Knightshayes. He had a passion for the Middle Ages and Gothic architecture which he interpreted in his buildings in the most colourful and exuberant manner possible. He was born in 1827 and died in 1881, having created some of the most dramatic interiors in Britain, especially for the fabulously wealthy Marquess of Bute at Cardiff. So when I saw The Gatehouse kit for sale in Dollhouse Emporium's catalogue in 2006 for £40, I knew it would be the perfect setting for a Burges-themed interior. I have put his initials on a plaque above the upstairs window. I made doors with a Christmas card bought from the very Gothic stately home, Tyntesfield, in Somerset. The top floor has a roof garden inspired by that at Cardiff Castle though that has a Roman theme rather than Egyptian, but I saw this colourful paper at the Georgian House Dollshouse Shop in Cardigan and it seemed appropriately exotic. However in the other two rooms the theme is purely mediaeval. In the bedroom I have used angel-patterned Christmas paper, with a gilded Taiwan bed with the bedhead scene (very characteristic of Burges) cut from a German chocolate wrapper.

Cutouts in *Dolls House World* magazine provided me with the Nonesuch type chests, the small one in the bedroom and the larger in the entrance hall, and I made the light fittings too from brass strip; and the gilded figure in the bedroom is a Christmas cherub ornament. The frieze in the entrance hall is inspired by that in Cardiff Castle Nursery and was photocopied from *The Anatomy of Costume*. I made the fireplace. The chair on the left is a model of the Coronation chair at Westminster Abbey, and the other was bought at Caldicot Castle. The decorative candleholders came from Teepee Crafts which specialise in miniature filigree metal work. Their catalogue was a standby for many years, one could seldom get near their popular stall at Miniatura! The occupants were added later, the elegant lady owner and the housekeeper downstairs were both bought at the Georgian Dollshouse shop in Cardigan.

William Burges gatehouse, the entrance hall.

VICTORIAN SHADOWBOX

Shadowboxes, as these shallow glass-fronted boxes are known, are in effect 3D pictures. One can buy new ones for display but they are expensive, I was lucky to pick up a rather grubby pair in a charity shop.

This is my favourite, the occupant represents a late Victorian grandmother, who is a peg doll dressed by me, (if one saws the legs off a peg doll, one can provide them with pipe cleaner legs so can be seated,) an Archdeacon's widow, in the heavy mourning popularised by Queen Victoria, but despite that she is rather a jolly person, with bright blue eyes, happy with her little dog. Making this charming little room setting was great fun, the walls are covered with Teepee frames containing family photographs. The glass-topped display table contains stray charms once available in miniature Christmas crackers. I assembled the sewing table from the top of an old cotton reel with its tiny compartments, and added an ornamental pedestal, inspired by one in Caroline Hamilton's *Decorative Dollshouses*, as was the curtain which frames the scene. Her tapestry work was cut from a battered old evening bag.

SAGAMORE HILL

This house was a 24th sale kit Fantasy Villa (from Maple Street) which I was given on the way home from our trip to Arnhem with JLB, Lin organised a quiz to pass the time on the coach and I narrowly won.

Its gingerbread appearance reminded me of old American houses seen near Angel's Flight in Los Angeles, and though rather more fussy, also bore a similarity to President Teddy Roosevelt's summer home Sagamore Hill at Oyster Bay, Long Island, with its downstairs verandah encircling the house and upstairs balcony.

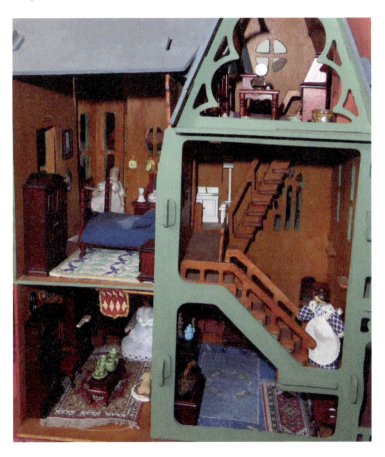

Having visited the Roosevelt house, its guidebook provided me with plenty of information to furnish the house appropriately. Teddy Roosevelt, though less well-known in Britain than his cousin Frankin Delano, is affectionately remembered for having established the principle of National Parks and also said to be the originator of teddy bears, having adopted a baby bear rather than shoot it!

He built the family summer-house in 1884 and it remained in his family till his widow Edith's death in 1948 when it was opened to the public. Obviously I could only recreate some of the rooms: the hall with its animal heads and Edith's drawingroom, and above that a bedroom and in the attic the Gun Room which was also the President's sanctum. I photocopied the gun rack in the book and reduced it in size. The nicely made period wooden furniture was acquired at Soest Dollshouse Fair and so were the smallscale dolls required for the house, Edith, the President and a couple of their boys, and the parlourmaid Clara. It was much easier to acquire one twenty-fourth scale dolls abroad at that time, especially adults. I immensely enjoyed making all the soft furnishings and the tiny carpets. Felicity Price provided some beautiful designs for miniature carpets. The resin garden furniture on the verandah was found in an Avon Catalogue.

Sagamore Hill

DUNHAM COCONUT HOUSE 1890s

The Dunham Cocoanut House as it is spelt in the USA where it originated, was the brainchild of the Dunham coconut processing company, who came up with the idea of turning the packing cases in which their packets of shredded coconut were shipped, into simple four-roomed dollshouses as an advertising gimmick. Four rooms were created with elaborately lithographed paper: kitchen, dining room, parlour and bedroom, and the exterior had lithographed stone walls and windows. Furniture could be obtained by sending in labels from the coconut packets. As you can imagine survival is rare and only a few houses are preserved in the USA and, as far as is known, only one set of furniture in the Ashburnham Historical Museum in Massachusetts. In October 1996, *International Dolls House News* devoted several pages to an article on this house with almost fullsize pictures of the litho'd walls and I was so charmed by the interiors which include a moose head and fish tank, as well as more usual items like a piano and kitchen dresser, I decided to try and reproduce the house myself. This was achieved with the assistance of the very helpful owner of Llun a Gair Art shop in Aberaeron, who colour photocopied and enlarged the illustrations. This was a tricky business because the side walls were not so clearly shown but by photocopying each room twice I got enough of the delightful designs to paper the 4 rooms. As the basis of the house I had discovered a three-fold small screen of compressed board in our garden shed, which a previous owner had thoughtfully left behind. I added a wooden base and made floors and a top from cardboard, covering the front edges with narrow strips of wood to look like the packing case's divisions. As my screen was a little taller than the original, I ended up with a lower fifth room which I made into an attic. I painted the exterior to look like stone and found some windows to photocopy among project designs in *Dolls House World* magazine in June 1999. The photocopies give a very faithful representation of the interior. As no illustrations of the furniture were available I furnished it simply but appropriately for the period, mostly with attractively painted green Taiwanese furniture which went well with the colour scheme, and experimented with crackle glaze as I had long wanted to do, on a Taiwanese side table, this gives a distressed look. There are no end of paint ranges and glazes available from acrylic paint suppliers. I made the armchair and sofa myself from padded cardboard, and the silk rug and flowerpot were a present from my Australian cousins. The kitchen stove is Sylvanian, from dollshouse furnishing created to house small animal families, then readily available. The dolls are especially charming. They were originally part of the much-maligned and expensive Del Prado "build your own dollshouse" with weekly magazines, which I did not collect, but if they are typical of the quality they really are extremely good, imitating 19th century porcelain dolls and exquisitely dressed. Mine were acquired at Clocktower Models for £9.50 each. The table mats are enchanting: tiny reproductions of Breton china patterns bought at Miniatura as was the well made food. Of course it would be wonderful to own an original Coconut House but I am very pleased with my adaptation.

My Dunham Coconut House, side and front views.

Dunham Coconut House, ground floor kitchen and first floor above.

Dunham Coconut House, second and third floor.

MITTEL EUROPA HOUSE about 1900

This charming little chalet-style kit house was found at the Salvation Army Reclamation Centre in Aberystwyth, known as CRAFT. Helen Palmer, the archivist at Aberystwyth Record Office, told me she had found a battered dollshouse there so I visited it once a month and found this in March 2004, already made up, for £5. There was no indication of the maker. A few pieces were missing: part of the roof of the porch and the fronts of two of the windowboxes, deficiences I made good with mount card. Like all the cheaper kit houses it has no back.

Although such a house would lend itself to a folk-art

treatment, I already had three buildings furnished in folk art style, so decided to furnish it according to photographs in *Mittel-Europa - Livng in Style in Vienna, Prague, Budapest and the Lands of the Danube*, by Suzanne Slesin and others, published by Thames & Hudson, 1994. The particular inspiration was a chalet-style country house in Lower Austria, (pp 227-235) whose interior was created by Josef Hoffman, leader of the Viennese avant-garde (Secessionists), in 1899, who knew of and admired the work of Charles Rennie Mackintosh and was influenced also by the English Arts and Crafts Movement. Obviously I had to adapt the ideas to a much smaller house and resolved to recreate the living-dining-room cum kitchen, the spa-inspired bathroom and the bedroom, as well as the staircase' banisters and the screen upstairs, with which I am particularly pleased, carefully made of painted cardboard. I filled the window boxes with pots of geraniums made of Fimo. The bathroom suite was acquired from a Hobbies catalogue. The chap came from Arnhem Dollshouse Fair and the beautiful lady doll was bought at the Georgian House Dollshouse Shop in Cardigan. The goblets and chocolate box were found at Miniatura. as were the flowers in the brass pot, a charity shop buy as was the china stove. I made the period coats hanging on the coat-rack from Shrinks' sewing kits for an Inverness coat and feather trimmed ladies coat acquired from Cassel's stall at Miniatura.

Mittel-Europa House

Mittel-Europa House

CHARLES RENNIE MACKINTOSH HOUSE

Charles Rennie Mackintosh has probably one of the best-known architects' names in the world. He was born in Glasgow in 1858 and died in London in 1928, where he was having treatment for cancer. He married a fellow artist, Margaret Macdonald, whose work was equal to his in designing avant-garde interiors, and of whom he said "Margaret has genius, I have only talent." His Glasgow School of Art was considered one of the finest buildings in Britain, and I have visited it, luckily before it has sadly been destroyed twice by fire. I have long admired their work so it was inevitable I should like to make miniature interiors in their style. The Dolls House Emporium advertised a superb miniature Mackintosh house based on several of his houses, but at £400 it was beyond my means. However, when I was in Hicksville, Long Island, I saw at their IKEA store, an elegantly simple, sturdy kit house with 2 rooms, for $39, and bought two, they have polished wooden floors and white walls. Curiously they had not been shown in the IKEA catalogue. When I returned home, and my son Guy saw them he said they were also available at their Cardiff store, so I acquired two more sets of rooms. Dolls House Emporium (and later the National Trust for Scotland) sold beautifully-made examples of Charles Rennie Mackintosh furniture and fireplaces, but these were generally highly priced, starting from £22. However, for a brief period before the deal with the National Trust, items were offered at half-price and I acquired a fireplace, wardrobe, the famous 'kimono' desk, a sideboard, tables and some armchairs. Otherwise I have made faithful copies of other pieces of furniture, like the double bed and dressing-table, and the cabinet in the bathroom, and his signature tall chairs, and soft furnishings including Charles' almost abstract roses, assisted by a timely series of articles in *Dollshouse & Miniature Scene* in July 2003 and *Dolls House Magazine* in August and September 2003. Another valuable source was Fanny Blake's *Essential Charles Rennie Mackintosh* which has superb photographs. I have also visited as many Charles Rennie Mackintosh houses as I can, including their own home interior recreated at the Hunterian Art Gallery, at the University of Glasgow, and Hill House in Helensburgh, whose hall carpet I painstakingly worked for the diningroom in my house. The Art Nouveau carpet in the little girl's room was an Elkie Grant of Carpet Matters design which seemed to fit, (*Dollshouse & Miniature Scene*, October 2002) and the bed is a copy of that at Hill House, worked by me. Thereby hangs a tale. Dolls House Emporium rather misleadingly sold a Mackintosh family, the children named Rona and Douglas, but the Mackintoshes had no children, they did have a nephew Sylvan McNair, son of Margaret's artist sister Frances and her architect husband

Herbert McNair. But by the time I acquired this information, which you can imagine was not as much in the public domain as information about their creative work, I had already provided the family. Margaret Macdonald was bought at a Christmas shop in Cold Spring Harbour, Long Island, and the little girl was a Heidi Ott (the renowned dollmaker) creation, but bought on a sale at the Toy Cave in Aberystwyth; Douglas (whom I re-dressed more appropriately) and Charles came from the same place. So I decided to retain them, as I had even provided Rona with a period dollshouse made of paper and photocopied from Olivia Bristol & Leslie Geddes Brown's wonderful book on *Dollshouses*. Douglas/Sylvan's room was furnished with an attractive set of Taiwan furniture painted white to match the rest of the house's furnishings and his dolphin carpet is another Elkie Grant design which I made. The 144th scale greenhouse (by In Some Small Way) was acquired as a kit at Miniatura and seemed a suitable toy for a Mackintosh relation. Adapting cheap modern items is something I often do, and my son Guy was adept at producing all sorts of items he'd come across including the very Mackintosh-looking hearth in the diningroom, which was bright orange originally! I photocopied a Mackintosh design for the rather startling dining-room walls. Finding a miniature architect's desk seemed unlikely and spying one through an office window in

Cardiff I was able to create my own from bits of kit furniture, and Dolls House Emporium supplied the drawings to go on the wall. Some of Margaret's artwork also appears in the house. I made most of the kitchen furniture and found them a maid Maggie, quite an early celluloid doll, dressed as she was when I bought her, but minus a leg, a deficiency I have made good. The kitchen houses a delightful collection of miniature items including a mixing bowl filled with cake mixture and a very Scottish Dundee cake made at a Dollshouse Club I used to attend in the old chapel at Pentregat when my friends Frances and Haydn lived there.

Mackintosh house, the architect's office.

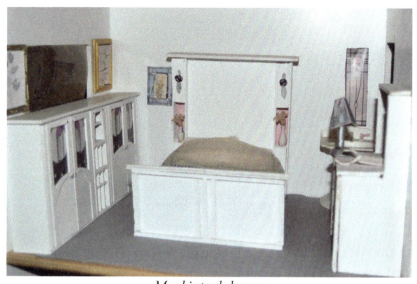

Mackintosh house

Mackintosh house

Mackintosh house

DEMEL'S BAKERY & CAFE

This foreign-looking shop, reminiscent of Continental buildings, was one of the first houses created by Mr Bob Martin when he retired and turned his hand to making them. I saw it priced at £45 in the window of his daughter's bakery in Barmouth, the shop was closed at the time and I was so charmed with it I arrived on the doorstep before opening time next morning determined to snap it up before anyone else!

He had designed it as a grocer's shop and provided a dresser and the counter at the back and modelled some food for the window. My inspiration was to make it into a patisserie like Demel's in Vienna with a cafe above.

Demel's was founded in 1897 by Gustav Demel whose portrait hangs in the cafe, - stuck on by Mr Martin, but given the handsome antique silver frame by me. The lady serving is dressed for that period and is a wax doll bought at a Criccieth bookshop along with the Spanish-looking customer in the cafe, at £6 each. Providing the many samples of cakes and boxes of sweets which fill the useful set of white shelves on the left was great fun, some are professionally made and beautifully decorated. There are Easter eggs and lambs such as are sold in Vienna at that time. The dresser has sugar blocks in the attractive packaging in which cafes abroad supplied them with one's coffee - to my surprise they have preserved well as have the ring doughnuts I made from a form of cereal coated with clear nail varnish. There are tiny paper bags too. The cafe is very fashionable as Demel's always has been, and frequented by poets, professors, and ladies of fashion but respectable enough for children too. You will find Sigmund Freud among the clientele. He is one of a series of famous figures reproduced in plastic some years ago by Accoutrements. The waitress is Elise, a modern plastic doll, who occupies the basic attic bedroom.

The decor is Art Nouveau - the mural in the shop is a photocopy of a mural in Prague which has many beautiful Art Nouveau buildings; and those in the cafe are postcards from the Victoria & Albert Museum. The very period bentwood chairs were actually an orange plastic "Little Lucy" set, painted black. As the tables are invisible beneath the check cloths (which has to be stiffened slightly with PVA and water to hang correctly) they are a collection of oddments. I made the slices of cake which appear on the plates.

89

Demel's

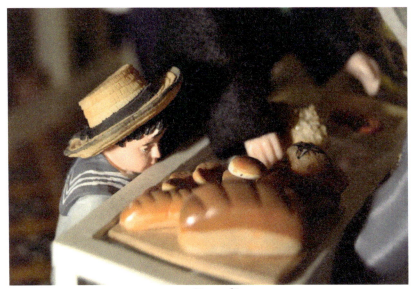

Demel's

PLACE DU TERTRE

Inspired by a number of miniature squares seen at the Paris Dollshouse Fair, I decided to make my own, named after my favourite square in Montmartre. The basis was part of a sturdy kit house bought at the Georgian Dollshouse Shop in Cardigan for £32. I used the sides and roof as I wanted a really solid frame. Card and sandpaper reproduced the facade of the original inspiration and Das was used to make the cobbles. The leaves on the real twig tree and blowing about the cobbles were also acquired at the fair. The cafe awning is made from a silver chocolate box wrapper and again copies one seen at the fair.

The table, chairs and artist's easel were made from patterns in an excellent little French book called simply *Miniatures*, by Isabelle Dorison, printed by Hachette, and also bought at the fair. The gent enjoying his breakfast at the cafe table, courtesy of a charming magnet bought at Calais in the terminal, is a cheap doll bought at The Parade in Shrewsbury. The slightly raffish lady chatting him up was found at a Dollshouse Fair at Hopetoun House in Scotland. The very French looking children studying the paintings are from Dolls House Emporium as is the artist, I made his hat. The artist's palette came from the Paris Fair and so did the water scene painting, exquisitely done.

I made the other paintings, all copied from the period, particularly the Davies of Llandinam collection at Cardiff; two are copies of watercolours I bought in Barbizon as a teenager: of the village, beloved by Impressionists, and the famous Moulin de la Galette in Montmartre. The balloons were found at Miniatura and so was the little artist's model holding them, on a secondhand stall. I later added the cats, and the waiter and baker (made and dressed by me) with his French loaves, another magnet bought at Calais. Though quite simple it is one of my favourite creations, keeping fresh, as it does, memories of many happy times in Paris.

SHELL VILLA

This was a former CD storage cabinet acquired in Barmouth, with its clapboard exterior and windows intended for pop star photos! This was recreated as Shell Villa, a boarding-house for cats, inspired by one owned by Vivien Greene. Vivien Greene, Mrs Graham Greene (1905-2003), who was one of the first people in Britain to appreciate the value of historic dollshouses and had a wonderful collection of her own displayed at the Rotunda, near Oxford until shortly before her death, was a familiar name to me from quite an early age since I was given her seminal book on *English Dollshouses of the Eighteenth & Nineteenth centuries* when I was about seventeen, and spent hours poring over the black and white illustrations. But she also had a more frivolous side, and one house in her collection she called the Haunted House and even set up a clockwork ghost in it and of course had the cats' holiday home. Sadly I never managed to visit the Rotunda but did get to Bonhams to view her collection when it was being sold. Her Shell Villa is Number 11 in the Catalogue of Part I of the collection. I arranged the shell patterns in plaster on the gables and added windowboxes made of lightweight card. The metal cats' heads on the exterior are buttons. However, it was finding a set of five miniature cats in Woolworths which gave me the idea of making the house.

Tabitha and Selina own the villa, and the guests are Mr and Mrs Blackie and the latter's sister Dimity. I have dressed all the lady cats appropriately. All the portraits are of cats and include a Felicity Price embroidered cat picture design which I worked for the house. The furniture is all modern but appropriate to the era of early in the twentieth century. I made the bed in the lefthand bedroom and the aspidistra in the dining-room and the salmon for supper.

GINGER & PICKLES SHOP

Everyone is familiar with Beatrix Potter's beautifully illustrated stories and when I came across this Wild West store in a junk shop, I could see it lent itself well for adaptation as Ginger & Pickles Shop, I only had to paint it green and make brick-paper covered cardboard bases for the bay windows.

There was no back wall, so I made one out of mount board and put tromp l'oeil shelves and cutouts of goods on them. The shop contains everything mentioned in the book, bacon and candles and red spotted handkerchiefs.

Although resin models of Beatrix Potter's most popular characters are readily available, so it was easy to find Peter Rabbit and Mrs Tiggy-Winkle, it took me a while to trace a suitable Ginger and Pickles and to find Samuel Whiskers too in scale. At Miniatura one can find many tiny items like the perfect little biscuit tins, candles and the slices of bacon, I cut the red spotted handkies from a fullsize scarf.

Ginger and Pickles shop, showing tromp l'oeil back wall.

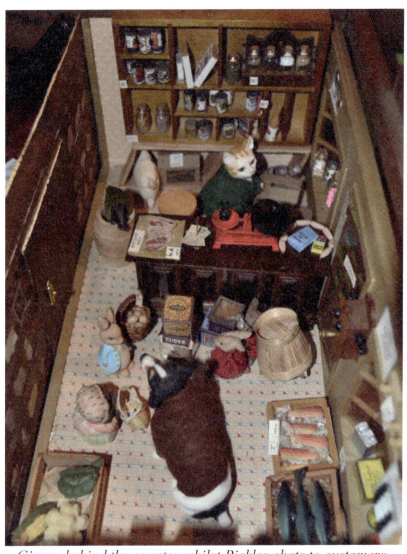

Ginger behind the counter whilst Pickles chats to customers.

Ginger & Pickles shop, Samuel Whiskers eyes the bacon.

Peter Rabbit and Mrs Tiggy-Winkle are customers.

CHARLESTON

When my friend Liz Parkin moved to Banbury to live with her daughter, she left me this kit house which she had bought for £19.99 at The Old Barn in Aberaeron. She had built it and painted the exterior but not finished it and stored it in her garden shed where it had got damp with some irremoveable stains so I had to paint greenery over it to disguise them. My first idea was to make it into a country cottage occupied by an artist but then I saw the clever recreation of Duncan Grant's studio at Charleston in Jessica Ridley's *The Decorated Dollshouse*. From 1916 Charleston was the Sussex home of the artist Vanessa Bell and Duncan Grant, who came to live with her there. They were part of what is known as the Bloomsbury Set, referring to the area in London where her sister, the writer Virginia Woolf lived. Vanessa was part of a group of artists calling themselves Omega, the name of a shop they had before WWI in London, selling their art work and decorated furniture. I made and painted the fireplace surround, table and screen following Jessica Ridley's designs, also the pottery and lampshades. I consulted Isabelle Anscombe's *Omega and After: Bloomsbury and the Decorative Arts* as well.

The larger colourful chair was made by Bob Martin for his Tudor House (see Cleddau Crafts) and the smaller flowered chair was made by Liz. The cats came from an

Andy Warhol calendar and the French books with their appropriate design covers were bought in Paris by my niece, the poet Samantha Rhydderch, whose photograph from the cover of *The New Welsh Review* also appears in miniature on the wall as she looks very 20s.

At the time I did not have pictures of the other rooms but decorated them as I thought fit. The attic contains miniaturised photos of Vanessa and her family and friends, and paper fans painted to Omega designs, as well as a bust I made of Fimo and a portfolio I made and filled with my own cut down sketches. The bedroom has exotic bedclothes made from folk embroidery and a copy of a late nineteenth century showerbath, like one seen at Erddig. I made it from thick, pliable wire and it has a tray in which you stand as water is poured over you. The kitchen is very basic as most of that era were but I amused myself by painting on the wall a rather weird seagod from an early sculpture seen at the Parthenon museum, which seemed just the sort of thing to appeal to the Charleston occupants.

Some time after creating the house, I visited Charleston which is open to the public, and was pleased to find how faithful my reproductions were. Unusually, the house seemed so complete in itself I never felt like providing inhabitants. That beautiful area below the Downs appealed also to Virginia and her husband Leonard Woolf, and they bought a cottage a few miles away in the village of Rodmell and Virginia often bicycled over to see Vanessa: there is a bicycle on the verandah.

Charleston

Charleston kitchen with 'seagod' painting.

Charleston

THE TEAPOT DOME: THE ROARING TWENTIES

This was inspired by photographs in *Sunset Magazine* which my mother received from her American cousins and which showed The Brown Derby in Hollywood, shaped like a Bowler Hat which the Americans call a Derby, which was a bar and dancehall. My son Guy found the Fisher Price teapot in a secondhand shop; it's original colour is bright yellow, and I painted it silver and mounted mirror card letters on a strip of card around the lid saying THE TEAPOT DOME.

The floor paper is Art Deco, photocopied from Ian Zacek's book *Essential Art Deco*, and with great difficulty

I lighted it. There is a bar, and the floor is crowded with flappers and their partners. And there is of course a band. These are mostly early 1950s child dolls which still turned up frequently at fairs, which I dressed appropriately, not forgetting to paint red hair on one, to represent the girl in the song *"Don't Bring Lulu!... Lulu has the reddest hair"*. The partition was inserted to make lighting easier.

STEAMSHIP OFFICE

This was suggested to me when I read Peter Jones' article Lettering and the Computer in *Dollshouse & Miniature Scene*, January 2001. He said *"Typefaces can encapsulate the atmosphere of different periods"* and one of the illustrations was for a Steamship Agency. The building on which various 30s typefaces were displayed looked like a corner shop, and as it happened I had been given a discarded corner shop by Eve when she was winding down the shop in Tywyn. It had been dumped on her by a customer who had intended to make it into a grocery store but wearied of the project. I had not wanted to make a food shop myself as already had the Ginger & Pickles shop.

There was a touch of filial piety about the Steamship Office as my grandfather James Gillies was Commodore of the Canadian Pacific fleet and later Managing Director, and my mother and her sisters spent many happy holidays with him on board ship. Between the wars was the great era of luxury cruising on liners like the *Normandie,* and the *Empress of Britain. Essential Art Deco* again proved an invaluable source which guided me in colour and style and even the lettering outside is a faithful copy cut from thin card. I painted the office cream and added silver swing-doors with 30s sunbursts.

I made the grey leather furniture on a polystyrene base. The leather-topped desks are made in Taiwan and perfect for the setting. The files on the shelves came from Bodleian Library postcards, this is a very easy way to fill shelves. The posters came from *Essential Art Deco* and the model ship is actually a pencil sharpener. I made the senior partner and his assistant, from Fimo, and note the cigar in the ashtray on the former's desk, and the electric fan, found at The Parade, Shrewsbury. The lady passenger needed elegant legs so I used a modern plastic doll but dressed her for the period with her cloche hat and arrowhead brooch. We have a photograph of my mother in just such a cloche hat, launching the *Princess Helene* in 1927. At first I made her a set of luggage down to a jewel box, but found better luggage at Miniatura with the Luggage Lady so the luggage was reused in the Corfu Villa (see below). She has a passport, first introduced in the 1930s. This too is a favourite creation.

The interior of the Steamship Office.

MAVIS BANK: AN ART DECO INTERIOR

This house was also acquired at the Salvation Army reclamation centre in Aberystwyth, known as CRAFT, and operating in part of the old Railway Station. I brought it home with great difficulty on the bus. Unfortunately it had been zealously "restored". The public at large obviously do not understand that old dollshouses are much more valuable to collectors in their battered state! From photos, Marion Osborne kindly dated the house for me to the 1930s with its roundheaded door and the Romside windows which swivel at the top. The external stucco has been overpainted, the stairs too in cherry-red enamel paint, and the rooms decorated quite nicely with handblocked papers. There were no internal doors so I have added these myself.

It is furnished throughout in 1930s style with some very interesting pieces. The bedroom suite was made in Japan, it is inlaid with a pattern in darker wood. Japan made lot of dollshouse furniture between the wars and it is very attractive and often quite reasonably priced even these days. I paid thirty euros for the suite which included the bedding with its beautifully made quilt. It was bought at the April Fair at Arnhem on a stall specializing in antique furniture. The wardrobe contains crocheted miniature clothes.

On the dressingtable are miniature items from Chrysnobon which I painted in tortoiseshell in imitation of thirties items. My mother possessed several tortoiseshell combs. I embroidered the bedroom picture and those downstairs, our house contains several pictures embroidered by my mother, and it was a popular hobby of the time. I also made the very thirties rug. There is a miniature kewpie doll by the bed. Kewpie dolls were derived from comic strip characters created by cartoonist Rose O'Neill in 1909, hugely popular, they were soon imitated in china and composition, like mine, which was bought at the Freeport Dollshouse Fair on Long Island. They remained popular for forty years being later made in celluloid, and in hard plastic in 1949. The bathroom suite came from a Hobbies catalogue, and its modernity suits the period. The Lloyd Loom linen basket was made by me from sewing canvas. The hall contains a set of Clarice Cliff china got at Miniatura. The sittingroom wall lights are scent bottle tops. The chair on the left is copied from a Frank Lloyd Wright design in *The American Miniaturist*, of April 2003. I made the Clarice Cliff design carpet from a pattern in *Dolls House World* September 1998, and the picture pattern came from *Dollshouse & Miniature Scene* in December 2002. The fireplace is a Barton 30s design bought from Ktminiatures for £7, and the mat before it is an Elke Grant abstract design. The sideboard in the sitting room and armchair with curved plastic sides came from Gunter Witt's stall at Arnhem, and this fair also provided the small girl which I dressed in a smocked frock such as I had as a little girl; but the beautiful, realistically dressed lady doll was bought at Soest Fair and so was the mahjong set they are playing with. It's simply marvellous with all its little pieces. Mahjong was a very popular game then, and I never expected to find it made in miniature but at Soest the unexpected is always materializing.

The 30s leather and metal sofa and chairs were bought at Pastimes in Glasgow, and are illustrated in Olivia Bristol and Lesley Geddes-Brown's book *Dolls' Houses*, described as in Bauhaus style, dating from the 30s. The table and bookcase, which look very art deco, were found at Carmarthen market. I made the books and magazines with appropriate covers. The Sunset cover comes from the original cover of 1929. The nameplate Mavis Bank was found at a small dollshouse fair in Falkirk, Scotland, and seemed to suit the house. Mavis is a Scottish word for swallow, and my mother's father came from Scotland, her older sister was named Mavis.

****

Little Grey Rabbit House

LITTLE GREY RABBIT HOUSE

The Squirrel, the Hare and the Little Grey Rabbit was published by Alison Uttley in 1929 and beautifully illustrated by Margaret Tempest, it was the first of many stories about the friends and other characters like Fuzzypeg the hedgehog and Wise Owl. I collected them all as a child and have them still. Once upon a time there was for sale a book with a cutout cardboard house for Little Grey Rabbit but the Mulberry Bush Bookshop, which specializes in dollshouse books, says it has long been unavailable. However I sent Bob Martin. who made my Viennese Cafe, a photocopy of the endpapers of the books which always show the exterior of the little house and a sketch of how I thought the layout of the interior would appear, as the only rooms illustrated are Grey Rabbit's and Squirrel's bedrooms and the livingroom. And he came up with an excellent facsimile of the house for £70. I had to make a false wall in the living room to conceal the staircase and create a pantry as appears in the book and have done my best to furnish it exactly as in the illustrations. It is striking that although the story is about country dwelling animals, the colours and carpets reflect the contemporary trends. I had to make or adapt a lot of the furniture and make the carpets - out of felt, and even print my own fabric, for the living-room armchair and Little Grey Rabbit's bed. Squirrel is a Sylvanian toy and

I have re-dressed all the animals to match the illustrations.

Little Grey Rabbit House

THE LARSSON HOUSE

It was quite difficult to decide whereabouts in the book to place this house, since it can, I suppose. be classed as collectable, being a Barton house called Claremont Chalet dating from 1981 bought at Eve's shop in Tywyn for £25 in 1999 and identified for me by Marion Osborne, in fact it's illustrated in her catalogue of Barton toys on page 72. In the 1970s Swedish-designed simple Lundby houses became very popular and this is very similar. It is therefore very appropriate to use it to create a Swedish-style interior. Lylla Hytnass, the original house on which this is based, was the home of Carl and Karin Larsson, artists, who had a tremendous influence on modern Swedish style, around the start of the twentieth century. The Victoria & Albert Museum devoted an entire exhibition to the Larssons' work, which inspired me to create this interior. I have long admired folk art which the Larssons also valued, I love Canal boat art and have had a go at Norwegian Rosemaling which is a similar technique. I have chosen to make the house occupied by Carl and Karin's grandchildren, still retaining the summer house's original decor and furniture. As I have mentioned earlier it is ill-advised to alter irrevocably any period dollshouse so I have created my interior decoration on card walls inserted over the original decor. I collect lengths of woven braid and patterned ribbons and they were very appropriate for adding a frieze round the top of the walls. The main bedroom is furnished with a folk art bedroom suite purchased at Kayserberg in Alsace and of course it has a duvet made in gingham.

The children's room contains small folk style pieces found at random and I made the 1930s Shell garage with which they are playing, a toy suggested by the miniature cars given by my son Lew. The livingroom has some beautiful pieces of pale green Japanese-style furniture found at La Courte Echelle in Brussels. Karin Larsson owned an almost identical display cabinet which she used for plants. The red sofa and coffee table are Swedish pieces from Stockholm, brought back by my son Guy.

The typical Swedish waisted grandfather clock is made by Lundby who produced a number of traditional style pieces. Beneath the stairs is a porcelain stove bought at Miniatura. The Larssons went in for strong green, red and yellow colours which is why I have used them in the sittingroom and kitchen and the lamps imtitate those made by Karin. In fact when the exhbition catalogue is placed alongside the house, you can see how faithful I have been to the original inspiration. The modern dressers in sitting room and kitchen were found in a fancy goods store, The Price is Right in Barmouth, such places often have items of imported furniture, and they and the Sylvanian sink unit were painted to match the decor as were the kitchen's chunky table and chairs from a plain wooden modern set of children's dollshouse furniture. I built the stove from a Phoenix Kit. The modern Mrs Larsson is a Hobbies doll and came with one of the boys and I found the other on a Rumanian stall at Soest. I made the flowers on the balcony from Fimo and pins, and the poster was part of a set of Swedish pictures brought from Stockholm by Guy.

My Larsson house kitchen and, below, one of the Larsson illustrations I used as colour reference.

CORFU VILLA - MY FAMILY AND OTHER ANIMALS

The Durrell family lived on Corfu from 1935-1939, and Gerald the youngest wrote very amusingly about this period in *My Family and Other Animals*. My friend Liz Parkin also passed on this house to me when she moved to Banbury in 2002. She said it was a Lundby house and it does have square doors but it has Barton characteristics too, the turned plastic banisters on the verandah are identical to those on the Larsson house and the plastic ornamentation on the landing is similar to that of other Barton houses, for instance the short-lived Super DeLuxe, so it may be a product of the period after Barton took over Lundby UK in 1984, although the firm continued to operate in Sweden. In fact Olivia Bristol & Lesley Geddes-Brown show an identical house which they say is Lundby, mine has obviously lost its facade. The imported wicker style furniture made in white wire became very popular in the 1990s and seemed appropriate to a holiday villa so I have used it extensively, but made the boys' and Margot's beds and Margot's room has heavy Victorian furniture which Gerald describes in one of the villas. As the family lived in India before Corfu I have used Madras cottons and Indian silk scarf material as bedcovers (the latter a relic of my hippy youth) and made the numdah rugs.

The Corfu House

I have tried to indicate the family's characteristics: Margot's dressingtable is cluttered with aids to beauty, these were very easily made from beads and small pieces of wood and I made the diaphanous dress hanging on the wardrobe. The tiny pairs of shoes come from Dolls House Enporium.

Guns hang in the boys' room for Leslie, and loads of home-made Penguin books on the shelf for Larry.

Alecko and the Magenpies.

Gerry's Magenpies and seagull Alecko are on the verandah, I made those too and the sea-snakes in the bath behind the blue and white striped curtains. I used Scenic water but was not very successful with it and replaced it with perspex.

Margot, Leslie in plus fours and fair-isle pullover, and Larry at the typewriter, are resin figures got at Maple Street through their catalogue, they billed themselves as the largest Dollshouse Shop in Europe and had a museum too at Wendy, Royston, Hertfordshire. Gerald and Roger the dog were found at Dolls House Emporium, and their friend Dr Theodore Stephanides was got in Soest and dressed by me as he is described in the book. I made the kitchen furniture and their friend Spiro, who has just brought Mrs Durrell some fruit. Mrs Durrell was found at Miniatura, undressed, with a porcelain head, arms and legs, and is dressed in 30s silk material which came from a great-aunt's dress. I made the cookery books including *Simple Recipes from Rajputan* mentioned in the book. The Durrells reluctantly left Corfu at the outbreak of war.

1940s HOUSE

I bought this house in May 2000 at the London Dollshouse Shop in Covent Garden, which as you might imagine was a very expensive place and I paid £135 for it - more than I ever have for any house before or since. But it is not as extravagant as it seems since small kit houses retailed then at about £85 and larger kits from £200-£400. Today the shop sells hand-made three-roomed houses for over £1000.

This house is very much influenced by contemporary Triang houses, with its gables, stucco walls and has commercially made Romside windows and door. The roof is unusual, being beautifully made of wavy strips of varnished wood and the porch roof is similar. It is back-opening and has a shallow board base.

At some time the facade has been overpainted and when I bought it the garden area was covered with an imitation stone paper which I picked off carefully to reveal the lawn and narrow brown-painted flowerbeds. This was done presumably to hide splashes of paint from the over-painting which I have touched up to match the original. Marion Osborne says it is definitely not a commercially-made house. The shop dated it as 1940s. But I fell in love with it because of its character and at that time it was the first older house that I owned. It has four rooms, a very narrow hall and landing, with a boxed-in staircase and in the livingroom a Romside tin fireplace. At some time in the 1950s a tromp l'oeil effect was created in the sittingroom by sticking in a dining-room scene from a magazine, which I have left in place though I have furnished it as a wartime house, complete with a Morrison's shelter in the room. Many people had an Anderson shelter in the garden, but some had one of these metal and wire mesh boxes in which to sleep indoors during the Blitz. I made it from a pattern in *Dollshouse & Miniature Scene* in November 1999, created by Rosie

Collard. The mesh on mine was cut from an ancient strainer, and the rest is cardboard. And of course there are black-out curtains.

1940s House, sitting room with Morrison shelter.

Most of the furniture dates from the 1940s: there is a charming Twiggs set in the main bedroom, bed, wardrobe and chest of drawers, and a Doltoi dressing-table; and a 40s wooden washbasin, and a Barton armchair got in Glasgow in the Argyll Arcade toyshop in 1947. The children's bedroom has a Doltoi wardrobe and two Doltoi bedside tables from the 1940s but they have lost their original drawers. The beds are small modern plastic ones as all the wooden beds were too big to fit in here.

The electric fire in the parents' bedroom is an exact copy of the one in my nursery as a child, I found it at Miniatura. I partitioned off the end of the landing by the window, to make a loo.

1940s House, the parents bedroom.

The Victory Loo Paper Rolls were cut-outs from *Dollshouse & Miniature Scene*. On top of the Morrison shelter are gasmasks made by Cassel's who made miniature ones for adults and children, and miniature ID cards and ration books were acquired too. The Camp Coffee printed cardboard box in the hall, made by Shepherd Miniatures, has been labelled SALVAGE. The armchairs in the sittingroom are made by Barton and the red painted table and matching chairs date from the 40s because I had them in my first dollshouse. I made the folding green baize-topped card table as they were much in evidence in all houses at the time with home amusements. My younger son sent me the miniature Monopoly board from America - during the war we played endless games of it. I made items like the radio and thirties mirror from projects in the same issue of

Dollshouse & Miniature Scene and the barbola mirror in the hall from Vivienne Boulton's delightful book: *The Doll's House Decorator*. The carpet is felt with a thirties pattern drawn in felt pen.

The kitchen has a Barton dresser known to be made by the 1950s, and a plastic Kleeware table, these were available in Glasgow in 1947. I made the ancient-looking stove from a Phoenix Kit. On it is a tiny tin tray of toffee apples, home-made sweets alone were available for much of the war. The sink is also metal with a plastic top, our sink which I remember as a new one just after the war was cream-painted metal with a stainless steel top. Rather to our amusement, its trade name was Elizabeth Ann. The Susie Cooper spotted teaset was again a suggestion of Vivienne Boulton's, and made in Fimo.

The dolls are a beautifully-made family of Grecon-style dolls such as I had as a child in the 1940s but were found brand new at The Set Piece in Barmouth in 2000 for £20. I have re-dressed the father as a naval officer. The only difference between them and my 1940s dolls that I can see, is that they have rather rudimentary wire feet not metal shoes. Grecon dolls were originally made by Margarete Cohn of wool covered wire. with painted faces, and woollen hair. In her *Barton Model Homes*, Marion Osborne devotes several pages to these iconic dolls which are still available secondhand although at high prices, as they were made for about 50 years from 1927. There are tiny perfectly-made copies of Arthur Ransome books just as I had in my childhood, made by Ktminiatures.

Naval Officer and duffel coat.

KIOSK

A Marklin 1910 tinplate newspaper kiosk just like this sold for £2,860 at Christie's. Cilla Dennis saw it and was fired to make one herself. Her successful project featured in the April 1999 issue of *Dolls House World*. Like her I found it irresistible and made one for myself out of mount card, and the newspapers etc were provided by cutouts in the magazine. Although the kiosk dated from 1910 the newspapers they actually printed were for 1945 so I have included the kiosk here. It was great fun to make and turned out very successfully.

RAILWAY WAITING ROOM

I saw one made by Catherine Lewis in *Dollshouse & Miniature Scene* in August 2001 and loved the idea. She made hers in a roombox but I chose to make mine in an old boxfile. They are perfect for a shadow box and one can cut a window in the lid if one wants to but I wanted to use the jolly postcard got as a freebie at Aberystwyth Railway Station, a typical poster of the Golden Age of Rail between the wars. If one wants to be able to open and shut the file it is useful to have one like this which closes by wrapping a tie round a metal stud on the side (top in my case). The toughest thing was removing the very powerful spring clip inside it. It was a fascinating little vignette to make. The lady passenger in her very 40s suit, was made by me from Coronet porcelain paste, one can buy moulds for the whole figure and make jointed limbs. Her outfit is made from felt and she is using a tiny compact (from Teepee Crafts) to remove the inevitable smuts from her nose. She is accompanied by a suitcase, and a cat basket, the latter got at Soest Dollshouse Fair as was the crate of chickens. When I was young boxes of chicks were regular travellers on the trains. Above her on the left wall is a poster for the Talyllyn Railway, one of the "Great Little Trains of Wales", a fridge magnet, a souvenir of one of many rides on this delightful little train.

The old box file turned into a railway waiting room.

The chap at the Ticket Office in his smart uniform came from Jacqueline Mink's stall at Soest. The ticket officer was found in the Georgian Dollshouse in Cardigan. His office shelves are liberally supplied with rolls of tickets, a cash box made from black Fimo with red paint pattern, with a little metal key (Teepee Crafts) and a railway lamp - actually a lamp from a novelty shop selling seaside souvenirs, and volumes of railway regulations. There is also an old fashioned wall telephone, a fridge magnet. I went a step further than Catherine by putting a picture of a steam train outside my waitingroom window.

****

1950s/1960s BUNGALOW

This ranch-type house, fashionable full-size in the USA from the 1950s and copied in Britain later, was discovered for £15 in 2003 at Aberystwyth market and brought home with some difficulty on the bus.

An American girl seeing me once getting on the bus with a bookcase, said "Your buses are amazing, I saw a guy with a lamb on the bus yesterday!" I must admit I have travelled with all sorts of things including a monkey puzzle tree (smallish but very prickly), the drivers are very tolerant on rural buses. This is a home-made house, very sturdy and opens at the front and the rear, the roof also lifts off and the tall yellow chimney isn't fixed but slots into the roof.

The kitchen floor had tiled paper but the rest of the house had thick clumsy pieces of real carpets. There was no furniture. It has all the right details, "picture" windows, and a "stone" fireplace to the roof in the sittingroom. I made felt carpets for the house patterned patiently in felt pen to look like 60s carpets. I chose mostly Plan furniture designed for children because its simplicity put me in mind of the G Plan furniture which became fashionable in the 50s, my sister refurnished her bedroom in it but stick-in-the-mud me remained faithful to my nursery furniture. Plan furniture is beautifully finished in plain wood or gaily painted, and I got my sets for the bedroom, kitchen, bathroom and livingroom from the Toy Cave at Aberystwyth, they cost between £8.50 to £10. I especially like the shower. I made the pretty shelf of bathroom accessories myself from a design by Joan Key who did many projects for Dolls House World over the years. And of course it has an Ali Baba linen basket, which originally held cocktail sticks.

Two views of the kitchen.

The lovely handmade shopping bag was found at Thame Dollshouse Fair organised by Ktminiatures. The rack of wine bottles is a fridge magnet.

I chose gaily patterned curtains for the kitchen though they should really have had flower and fruit scenes on them, the other curtains have leaf patterns, very popular at the time, and I painted the rims of the diningtable china myself, in felt pen, to match a dinner service my sister was given as a wedding present in 1964. The blue glass bottles ranged along the window were bought in Brighton and are a very period fad.

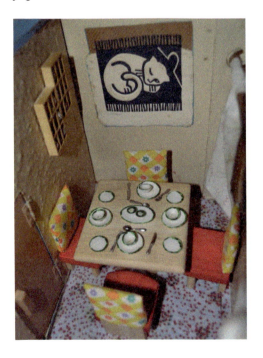

I found a couple of wonderfully Swinging Sixties pieces of furniture on Dieter Rose's stall at Soest fair, he specialised in them: the modern whatnot and magazine rack. The posters were chosen to suit, we were all fans of Jean Cocteau films in the 50s. I made and dressed the peg doll lady in her trouser suit and the chap was bought at Soest.

I made the transistor radio - *Dollshouse & Miniature Scene* December 1999 had a whole lot of marvellous 40s and 50s projects. I added records and games and the record-player and speakers came from The Parade in Shrewsbury. One of my favourite things in the house is

Sally Meekins' ceramic cat; she had a stall at Miniatura. It sits in front of the TV. The log basket is made by Lundby.

In the hall there is that 50s icon, a scooter, I remember dashing round London on the back of one, seated side-saddle and helmetless! There is also a duffle coat with tiny toggles, made by me from an excellent Shrinks (Cassel) pattern, and an Afghan coat! They hang on one of those atomic style wallhangers (I have a fullsize one still, and made this from Fimo.) The bedroom has some fashionable undies I made: a boned bra using plastic pill bubbles and a suspender belt, the design was shown in *Dolls House World*, November 2000. Also a tiny Pifco hairdryer. *Dolls House World* magazine in February 2000, offered the project of a hippy shop called Trends, whence came the carrier bag, one of their cut-outs.

FENTON TOWER

This 24th scale house with a plain single gable facade was acquired at the Dollshouse Fair at Hopetoun House in April 2005. The maker was Gordon Miniatures of North Shields, and it cost £25 which I thought was very reasonable for a solidly-made house with (plastic) windows and door, no staircase.

I had for a long time been thinking of building a Scottish tower house having seen some wonderful ones in pictures and inspired too by the real life pink-harled Fenton Tower near North Berwick. The pink harling was achieved by mixing washed and dried sea sand with tinted white emulsion and I made and carefully coloured the purple roof slates, also cutting the stepped gables. The tiny round towers were modelled in DAS and topped with conical roofs of handpainted cardboard slates. Because it is a castle the interior has rough stone walls using a paper got from Hattonwoods who also provided the 3D floor paper for the kitchen of stone flags.

The miniature furniture in the sittingroom came chiefly from Townhouse Miniatures, and the dolls are two oldish German dolls from Ilona Stahl's stall at Soest:

one is celluloid, the other pottery with wire joints. Mr Campbell was dressed by me but Mrs Campbell wears an exquisitely crocheted dress got at Miniatura. Note the tiny bellpush on the left.

Fenton Tower, the kitchen, note the brass dining table and chairs.

The kitchen was trickier to furnish but I gradually acquired the pieces. The stove is a 24th scale Kleeware and Townhouse Miniatures provided the fridge, the sink unit was found on Felicity Price's stall at Miniatura and the brass dining table and chairs to a Charles Rennie Mackintosh pattern came as a flat pack from PPD Ltd of Lochgilphead, Argyll, one bends them into shape. Grizel, the "daily" at the stove, is an inexpensive but nicely made plastic doll found at Soest, and dressed by me. The bedroom is furnished with elaborate cast resin furniture available from Avon but this set was sold at Miniatura. I embroidered the carpet. Penny Toys provided the towel rail in the bathroom and the rest are tiny china items found in Miniatura: bath, loo, and basin, boxed-in by me; and the sofa found in a fancy goods shop, also the porcelain telephone in the sittingroom.

Fenton Tower, the bedroom.

Fenton Tower, bathroom in the eaves.

CAIRNGORM CASTLE

This was built for me by Bob Martin, working from a photograph of Vivien Greene's castle of the same name, sold at Bonham's in December 1998 for about £1,000. I have a copy of the sale catalogue as I went to the viewing. It describes it as an impressive six-roomed Scottish baronial castle on two levels with a tower; representing the style of the late 19th century. Like Fenton Tower it is an old house occupied by a present-day family.

Cairngorm Castle, with Minty just visible at the base of the tower.

I really appreciated Bob's work, he confessed the

tower was very hard to accomplish and he did a great job for £70. He always set the prices. He enjoyed the commissions very much and even made the beautiful 4 poster bed for me as a present, it came with the house.

The top of the tower was plain but I was delighted to find the weathercock at Miniatura. There was only one floor in the tower in the original, but I added another from mount card, so that it provided Minty's bedroom, a bathroom and study for Adam Gillies, Minty's father, her mother is Catriona, and Gillies was my mother's maiden name, Adam and Catriona are Gillies family names.

Like Mrs Greene's castle there were no interior doors or staircase. Minty's furniture had to be very light in consequence: the modern brass bed came with its pretty check bedclothes and the pink plastic wardrobe, very nicely made with interior shelves as well as hanging space, is stamped 'made in West Germany' and carries the trade name Jean. The sheepskin rug came from the Orkneys and was sold at the village hall in Stronsay. All the lamps are made from half ping pong balls, an idea got from Caroline Hamilton's *Decorative Dolls Houses.* Minty herself, appropriately dressed in riding gear, is a resin figure and stands outside the tower with her adorable pony who is actually a fridge magnet. We have always been keen riders but only on other people's horses! The bathroom is a modern china set. I especially enjoyed organising Adam's study with its roll-top desk, (made in Taiwan) and family portrait made by me, the portraits throughout the house are from an illustrated diary of miniatures, and the frames were made from gold painted card and string to give the effect of mouldings. I have enjoyed adding items over the years, the safe is a pencil sharpener, like the model vessel in the Steamship office. Golf clubs, fishing rod, binoculars and camera were found at Miniatura as was his brief case, and the box files and official documents were cutouts from *Dolls House World.* The green wellies were removed from a National Trust keyring. The damascened sword hanging on the wall is a superior Spanish cocktail stick; and the cutlasses and pieces of armour were from my children's toybox. I made the desk calendar. Catriona and Adam's bedroom is panelled in white, inspired by a similar bedroom in the famous Uppark dollshouse. Apart from the bed already mentioned, the furniture is simple slot together wooden pieces. On the skirted dressing table, made from an old lace edged handkerchief, stand family photos, literally, I have used contact prints of my family. The tissue box made from a bead was an idea of Joan Key's from *Dolls House World.* The only fairly modern portrait in the house over the plain fireplace made by me is Picasso's painting of Gertrude Stein in a bought picture frame. I am a great admirer of both. The other painting is of the Scottish heroine Flora MacDonald. I have gone to town on the Scottish theme in both the upstairs diningroom and downstairs sittingroom, lining the walls with tartan hand kerchiefs and making curtains for the whole house in tartan.Hunting Stewart upstairs and Royal Stewart downstairs.

The very elaborately pleated curtains for the diningroom and sittingroom with their draped pelmets were inspired by real life curtains in Stately Homes. The elaborate plaster fireplace and plaster decoration along the cornice were made by Sue Cook and bought bit by bit from Eve's shop in Towyn as it was quite expensive. The dining table and chairs are beautifully made reproduction and inexpensive Regency, and I embroidered seat covers for the rather bristly grey velvet original cushions, using a Victorian design from Sue Hawkins: *Embroidered Projects*. The table is laid with paper plates I painted in red and gold designs, with modern cutlery and tiny plastic bowls, the oldest item is the decanter which was bought in 1947 in Argyll Arcade, Glasgow. The toast rack is solid silver made by Simply Silver, the only piece of their beautiful work I could afford. The side tables with serving dishes were made by me with marble tops from sticky-backed Fablon and using embossed wallpaper. I enjoyed making the raised pie from Fimo and the tureen contains green peas, a nightmare to make as so easy to lose. The glass cabinet and elaborate cupboard with a miniature punchbowl are Taiwan pieces. The glass cabinet contains tiny models made in Fimo, copied from Assyrian exhibits at the Ashmolean museum: the sort of thing an ancestor might have collected, I remember being shown a brick from the Great wall of China! Also tiny china bird ornaments found at Miniatura. On the top is a plastic model of an eagle. The gong was found at The Parade, Shrewsbury. I made the fish in a glass case displayed above it, the tiny clear plastic boxes used for cheap jewelry are ideal for this.

The sofa and armchair were bought by me in Argyll Arcade, in 1947, there is another armchair but it would not fit in the room. Their original blue covering was still as good as new but I have covered them with tartan as being more appropriate. The elaborate overmantel and fireplace is a modern reproduction, but I have inserted a beautifully made brick fireplace owned by me since 1950. The book cases are simple kit pieces, stained, and all the books were made by me from a Mini Mundus kit of 60 printed book covers, each book individually cut from balsa. The busts are of Queen Alexandra and King Edward, from Maple Street. The portrait over the sofa is of King James I of Scotland and First of England. The pretty painted table was found in Barmouth and holds bottles with real whisky! Given by my younger son who lives in Scotland. I therefore provided Catriona and Adam with glasses which I filled with clear nail varnish touched with a little gold paint. I had a frisson next day when I found the glasses empty! But it had evaporated and the mixture proved more durable next time.

Adam & Catriona are inexpensive dolls got at the Toy Cave, dressed as they are now. Above Adam hangs a plastic framed picture which I had when young and the tiny ornaments on the overmantel came from my own collection as a child, apart from the clock which, like the barometer, was found at Miniatura. The globe is a pencil sharpener, made by the same people as the safe. The deer's head came from the USA. I assembled the rudimentary armour displays on the wall from buttons and metal pieces and made the polar bear rug.

I made the red kitchen floor tiles from cardboard, painting them with the stuff I used to brighten up my own kitchen tiles. I love the Aga, it was always the centre of our house when young, producing a wave of warmth as you came in on cold nights. The rest of the furniture is modern too and I made the table. The mixer is a fridge magnet and I enjoyed collecting the bits of copper and china. Particularly charming are the eggs in a bowl waiting to be whisked by a tiny whisk and the box of miniature assorted cheeses. There is also an old example of Triang food, a salmon steak on a plaster plate. Janet, the daily, made by me, presides over the kitchen and is based on the characterful housekeeper in *Dr Findlay's Casebook*, a TV programme we enjoyed so much. Old style "bells" hang in the corner of the kitchen and were adapted from fittings.

Cairngorm, the kitchen and bedroom.

SUE'S TOY SHOP

This was one of my most fun projects. The wooden facade with its tall windows and swing doors, was bought at Miniatura and I provided a box back for it. I chose to paint it sugar pink and put matching pink striped paper inside. It has old-fashioned toys but makes no pretence at being historic like the kind of shop illustrated in *Mrs Molesworth: A Flat Iron for a Farthing*, or that you can see today at Pollock's Toy Shop in London. The shop fittings were bought at Dolls House Emporium. The dolls are an interesting collection, most were found at The Set Piece in Barmouth and were possibly made in China, but dressed for the Western market, sometimes a bit oddly like the small boy in silk tam and braid edged trousers and the lady behind the counter in a lace mob cap. But they are very well made, china with moveable limbs. The tall girl in charge of the children is artisan-made in glazed porcelain like a Victorian doll, and was found at the Parade, Shrewsbury, it was made by a local lady named Hazel and beautifully dressed. I most enjoyed of course collecting its tiny contents and this was done over time. The charming Victorian frieze, the Golden Primer, was got at the Bodleian Library. I had a few miniature items to begin with: the dollshouses are china souvenirs bought on childhood travels with my parents, like Shakespeare's Birthplace and Dove Cottage. I made the Noah's Ark and the toy theatre from cutouts. Some were not destined as toys - like the silk figures of a matador and senorita which were originally a brooch. Some of the most charming came from Soest: miniature versions of the wooden pull-along toys made in the Erzebirge region for centuries. My twice yearly jaunts to the Miniatura Spring & Autumn Fairs usually produced some new item. My only regret is I did not make it front opening, because it was not possible to hinge the heavy front to cardboard, so it is accessible only from the top, which makes it hard to photograph.

Sue's Toy Shop

THE GABLES: DRESS SHOP

I saw this pretty Hobbies kit at Tinytown in Blaenau Ffestiniog, a favourite port of call when I lived in Dolgellau. It was £41. Simultaneously I saw the exquisite frock Pat, the owner of the shop, had made freestanding, which now graces the upstairs of the shop, which has no back like most such kits, and decided I must have both and would make a dress shop. This again was a project with infinite possibilities. The simple counter and the pretty resin sofa and chair were bought at The Set Piece, Barmouth, along with the mirror, and the glass-fronted cabinet with its rolls of material, added by me, came from Maple Street. The hats were found at Miniatura as well as the parasol, and the shawl is by Miss Margaret. I made the frocks hanging near the door and the screen behind which to try on clothes. Finding the right, lightweight materials is always tricky, and I pounced with glee on a torn pair of American underpants discarded by my younger son, for the check dress! I also made the corsets displayed in the counter from stiffish white silk ribbon and narrow blue ribbon and braid got at Miniatura. Dolls House Emporium supplied the tiny cotton reels but the minute button display was produced by the Set Piece after I had said that I wanted some. The tiny pair of gloves came from a Card Craft shop. The basket contains miniature silk roses still available in haberdasheries today, like the pearl-trimmed bows. The engraved fashion-plate was a dollshouse magazine cutout as is the box on top of the materials cabinet; the enamelled fans on either side of the fashion-plate are earrings. I made all the dolls from pegs, wigs were found at Miniatura for the dressmaker-owner Miss Mehitabel, and customer, and I made the assistant's hair, she can kneel down working on Pat's dress, because I have sawn off the peg legs and given her pipe cleaner ones, like her arms. The pin cushion is made of blue tack. The date is roughly 1875.

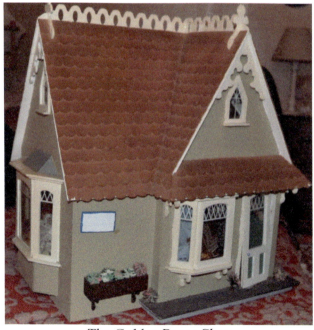

The Gables Dress Shop

The Gables Dress Shop, the dressmaker-owner Miss Mehitabel holds a corset. On the counter, cotton reels and a tray of tiny buttons.

CLEDDAU CRAFTS

This wonderful Tudor house was built by Bob Martin when he retired, and displayed in the window of his daughter's baker's shop in Barmouth together with the Viennese Cafe mentioned above. I have told there how hooked I was and bought both the very next morning when the shop opened, having to hire a taxi to get them home.

It is conveniently made in 3 separate floors which slot together, and cost £55. I thought it an absolute bargain when I discovered that even Tudor kit houses were £200 and his has mullioned windows and delightful winding staircases going up from each floor. He did - almost - spoil it by painting rather dauby fireplaces on each floor and sticking sacking it seems irretrievably on the floor. It was partly because of the sacking that I decided it should be a shop, one of those lovely tall Tudor houses in Shrewsbury that cater for tourists.

I love folk art and painted furniture and at the time American painted furniture was available relatively cheaply at Eve's shop in Towyn. But the very first item that went into the house was a miniature working loom bought in the fancy goods section of a local newsagent, hence the name of the shop: Cleddau Crafts as they made the little loom.

About this time I spotted the cheerful Woodentops and decided they would run the shop, they are named George and Martha Washington, two Americans who fell in love with Shrewsbury on their honeymoon and settled here. Shrewsbury is one of our family's favourite places and a day out there by train was a family treat from the children's earliest years. The upright spinning wheel must be over 100 years old and belonged to my Aunt Sue, born in 1898. There is a fabulous old metal cash register, actually a pencil sharpener. The pink settle on the 2nd floor and the blue cupboard and four poster bed on the top floor were bought from the maker on her tiny stall at Caerleon market. I am constantly adding items to it and it is a useful "shop" for other dollshouses requiring bedding. I painted the canal art tubs, from plain wooden ones got at Miniatura whence came the minute knitted items and I painted and decorated plain terracotta flower pots. Card makers craft shops have been a useful source of tiny items too.

    There are miniature catalogues I have made with cut outs of dolls house furniture in them. I made the only customer too, she is a peg doll dressed in a Joan Key creation found in Dolls House World in April 2000. Joan's wears a red mackintosh but I dressed her in red felt. It even has a tiny mouse who normally lives on the skirting board downstairs, given by my niece Samantha. It is one of the houses I always decorate for Christmas.

Cleddau Crafts, decorated for Christmas.

ANTIQUE SHOP

This was advertised in the local freebie paper, by Eiddwen Jones, Penralltwen, who had a stall in the Car Boot Sale in New Quay, under the name Betty Boop! I bought it for £30, because I liked the well-made shop window though the rest of the home-made house was a little unprepossesing, being back-opening with rather low-ceilinged rooms.

It had been covered in brick paper and I left that in situ and the grey tile paper on the roof. I am very pleased with the burglar alarm I made, copying a local one exactly, and further embellished and broke up the rather bare front of the house with a 2D metal postbox and a downpipe made from a black bendy straw. I had great fun creating really elaborate interiors, as I had some beautiful scenic wallpapers from Hattonwoods, bought because I could not resist them even though at the time I had nowhere to house them, with hunting and landscape scenes, which the shop also advertises for sale in the hallway with samples.

The house was originally simply painted white inside: walls and floors. I boxed in the staircase which emerges in the bedroom, panelling it carefully and although you can buy parquet patterned floorpaper, I went to the trouble of laying individual planks of stripwood stained, in the bedroom which is papered with the lovely landscape pattern. The carpet is a bright folk embroidery mat. The real lace curtains were cut from the borders of old handkerchiefs. I inherited dozens in fine lawn but all have now been used for bedding and other soft furnishings.

The bed was made by my friend Liz Parkin and I added bedclothes and gilded a sofa bought from Hobbies, and upholstered it with some silk patterned ribbon. On it sits Sophie Tyrwhitt-Price, a resin figure from *Dolls House World* Craft Club, her husband Cyril from the same source is downstairs in the shop, as soon as I saw them I knew they were ideal. The table by the bed has a cover touching the ground, very country house style, and the photos on it are family contact prints in Teepee frames. There is a davenport alongside Sophie with a rubber typewriter on it as Sophie keeps the accounts. And a radiator. The furry cats were a present from my niece Sami and I found their super climbing frame at Soest made by Barbara Welt.

The bathroom is floored in turquoise sticky-backed paper which gives the effect of linoleum and is wallpapered with small tree pattern on a pink ground. The chunky white bathroom suite came from Dollshouse Emporium, but the room is enlivened by fabulous sparkly green chiffon curtains, and a pink woodenframed Indian mirror with gold paint decoration. I have added a resin pink Lloyd loom chair, beautifully modelled. and a tallboy I made from a Chrysnobon kit. My favourite thing in the room however is an inch high shadowbox of a lady in a bath made from a pill bubble, an idea copied from Ronnie Godfrey.

My favourite room is probably the kitchen: I used red and white check tile paper on the floor. One wall is entirely covered with a printed cotton scene of an American country store, again bought long before I had anywhere to put it, from a craft shop at Aberaeron. The beautiful stove, a metal copy of an early 20th century one cane from the Craft Club too. The green kitchen chairs are resin with wicker seats. The dresser is a children's slot together kit piece stained and decorated with paper and filled with Delft-type china, always available at Miniatura. The wellmade sink unit and its drainer came from Doll House Emporium.

The shop has been carpeted throughout in a hound's tooth tweedy patterned but lightweight material, I have several times used it for men's suiting, for instance in the Steamship Office. The shop has many tiny treasures, exquisite porcelain, even souvenir china, a miniature Chinese lantern, a resin Queen Anne Dollshouse, Italian-made decorative mandolines, and small ornamental boxes, one has an inlaid brass duck in its mahogany lid. My favourite item is a real antique: an Arts & Crafts repousse pewter box with glass "jewels" set in the lid, a family heirloom. I must not forget to mention Rollo the alsation who reinforces the burglar alarm.

THE MOUNT: A TRANSFORMATION

This is an intriguing house, if ever there was one. It was bought at The Mount Antiques Warehouse in Carmarthen for £17 together with a few rather battered items of Barton dollshouse furniture.

The Mount, as found.

As you can see from the photograph taken when I got it home, it had been crudely painted in black and red, I tried removing some of the paint but could find nothing beneath but basecoat. It stands on a shallow green base, rather crudely painted green over white. But with the fronts open it looks like an older house as the rose patterned wallpaper found in most of the rooms is very similar to that use in Lines dollshouses - the predecessors of Triang. The bathroom had a blue tiny flowered wallpaper. Most floors were bare and stained, there had been paper on the sitting-room floor. The front of very thick wood seems like an unfinished later addition, no attempt had been made to decorate it and though holes were cut for the windows, nothing for the door. There were traces of sticky tape around the windows. The hinges look new. The staircase is well made and possibly commercial. It had a single chimney.

The Mount, restored.

I resolved to restore it to something like its Triang contemporaries. Strips of black painted card gave it some Tudor timbering on the bare gable and the facades were covered in washed sand and cream paint to give a stucco effect, I carefully brushed on greenery with a touch of pink on either side. The Romside windows and door came from Pastimes in Glasgow. The nameplate The Mount came from Sussex Crafts. It is furnished with some of its original furniture and other mostly period pieces.

There is a Barton pink and black bath in the bathroom, a Barton loo and dressingtable, and Lundby basin which was originally yellow but painted to match (with washable paint). The tiny towel rail is 1940s. The bedroom holds mostly the original Barton furniture with a Barton bed got at Pastimes. The cupboard on the right is modern plastic.

The sittingroom has a Doltoi fireplace, and above it hang pictures I made - copies of ones which appear on Marion Osborne's CD of 50s and earlier items. The lamp is Kleeware and the red settee and armchairs are by Barton. There is also a Jenny's Home (Triang) book case from the 1960s. The grand piano was probably made in Hong Kong. I embroidered the carpet and the staircase runner. The dolls are a Grecon doll bought at S W Golland's stall for £6, she lacked her dress but was otherwise in quite good condition retaining her metal shoes; and Doltoi children got at Pastimes. In the kitchen the stove is Sylvanian and the dresser, fridge and pots and pans were made by Barton and came from Pastimes too. The wooden table and chairs were in the Mount and date from the 60s and 70s, they are made in Czechoslovakia I think. The tart on the table in its frilly pie dish was made by me in a beer bottle top, they make neat dishes.

THE SMUGGLERS' INN

In October 2003 *Dolls House Magazine*'s cover carried an intriguing illustration of a mysteriously-lit Smugglers' Inn built on a rock with a cave beneath it, designed by Lesley Goodall. The pattern to create it proved quite simple if messy, as the rock is created from papier mache topped by a couple of cardboard boxes. Lesley Goodall used a flour and water paste for her papier mache, to soak the newspapers, but I found that PVA watered down was much less messy. One needs a lot of newspapers but it is great fun modelling the cave at the base of the structure, you need to leave a hole at the top of the cave for the smugglers' secret passage into the Inn's cellar whence another trapdoor leads to the Inn itself.

Smuggler's Inn: The basic structure.

It rests on a sand-covered cardboard base, easily achieved but make sure if using sea sand that it is washed and dried first or the salt will corrode the surface. Spread it thinly with glue and shake the sand all over it and any surplus can be shaken off and carefully collected for patching or re-use in other projects. The cellar is covered in realistic stone paper from Hattonwoods and partly by papier-mache too. It has a false wall to conceal smuggled goods.

The greenery clinging to the rocks is railway modelling material. I made ladders rather appropriately of driftwood to connect the three stages inside. The exterior staircase is a commercially-made one, and the rope banister is held in place by wire uprights. The basic Inn furniture came from the very good Readers' Digest *Family Book of Things to Make and Do*. As the Inn would be grubby I rubbed ash into the wooden floor boards. The perspex windows too are greenish.

It took some time to collect the brown glass bottles on the shelf and stoneware jugs, all were found at Miniatura. The resin figure keeping watch on a bench at the window was acquired at Picturiana, a local shop selling maritime inspired items which also supplied the well-appointed smaller boat for £4. I had to pay £10 for the handmade boat from Seaside Miniatures. Curiously the hardest thing was finding sizeable barrels, but eventually they turned up at Miniatura. I redressed porcelain dolls acquired at Miniatura also for some of the smugglers. My son Guy supplied one model with a knife in his teeth! The roof was roughly slated in cardboard and greenery applied here and there. It was made primarily to amuse my grandsons and has been well played with over the years by many visiting children as well.

Smuggler's cave!

SEASIDE SCENE & STALL

I had always admired elaborate beach scenes made by Dollshouse Clubs which featured in magazines and sometimes at Miniatura, so created a small one of my own in a sandfilled tray based around the pretty little tin hut found at Granny's Attic in Tywyn, for £3.

Seaside Scene, on an old serving tray.

The accessories were gradually collected, the little resin figures were bought in Barmouth, the larger doll in charge, from the Price is Right, attired as she appears in sundress and straw hat. The fish & chips & ketchup she is eating, so quintessentially British, were actually bought at Soest Dollshouse Fair! I am particularly fond of the rubber duck, a bathtub toy. Finding buckets and spades was tricky, the very small rubber buckets were made by Cassel's, the larger plastic ones were found at Soest. At Miniatura some years later I found the picnic stove and its bottle of gas. I made the paper picnic basket and contents modelled on one owned by us when young. The paper was the lining of a letter from my bank. This is on permanent display in my bathroom and always gives pleasure.

Seaside Stall.

The stall was bought as a kit on Seaside Miniatures' charming stall at Miniatura for £20. The striped material was not sold by them but used as part of their display and they kindly sent me a piece from their stock after the Fair. Most of the items on display were made by me, except for the buckets and spades, acquired at C & D Crafts at Miniatura who sold identical plastic buckets to some I had already but much cheaper than elsewhere, and the straw hats and one windmill to copy. This was a delightful project, I made the small wooden boats, and modelled the rubber rings from Fimo, and also made sandals and sunglasses from Fimo displayed in shallow card trays. I made a couple of windbreaks so essential for the British summer, from scraps of cloth and cocktail sticks, and modelled the balls hanging up in the net, saved from fruit. The postcards are my own contact prints kept over the years. The shrimping nets, and sticks of rock were made by me too, the latter from Fimo and patiently wrapped in cling film. I later acquired a lilo for only £1 on a charity stall at Thame Dollshouse Fair, and the lovely surf board from Seaside Miniatures, and could not resist the woven shopping baskets found at another fair even though the stall was really almost overflowing. I made the lady proprietress from Coronet porcelain paste, and added the small children, their bathers are miniature versions of those worn by my sister and myself early in the 1940s. The smallest is a rare old celluloid doll, the others modern porcelain with articulated limbs.

BACKSTAGE

This was another project inspired by Lesley Goodall, in Dolls House Magazine, December 2002; which she called 'At The Moulin Rouge'. Hers was made in a slightly larger boxfile, but I had been given a smart new red one so used that. She gave very detailed instructions for everything from wigs to the chaise longue. It is a very simple construction with a wooden upright to demarcate the wardrobe area from the dressingtable, just a shelf wedged in with a mirror. This must be at the right height for a seated doll to see herself in it. I papered the mirror surround with a pretty Japanese paper found at a Craft shop. I did not venture to make wigs, but made feathered headresses like the Bluebell Girls used to wear and these are on beautifully carved miniature hatstands found at Miniatura, which also supplied the black mesh tights. The plastic tiara supporting one of the head-dresses is, I think, from the Barbie Doll collection. I often bought odd Barbie garments in charity shops, as the materials were just the right scale for re-use in a dollshouse setting. The stool was made from a film canister covered with cloth and I padded the top, it matches the chaise longue, made from cardboard and balsa, the material has tiny musical notes on it. I put lights in by the mirror as an extra appropriate feature. I had great fun making costumes, as elaborately as I could and particularly like the black tutu.

Full size furniture braid provided the drop curtain along the top of the wardrobe area and a bamboo skewer made the hanging rod. The tiny coat hangers came from Miniatura, though I have made my own from twisted wire.

I found chenille yarn for the boa as Lesley suggested, and added a pink feather fan, and a spare pair of resin ballet shoes from Dolls House Emporium. The two dancers were found at the Georgian Dollshouse shop in

Cardigan and are beautifully made modern porcelain dolls, the latter by Wonham. Lesley used a re-figured plastic screen, found frequently in fancy goods shops, with her display but I made mine from mount card with mirror card on one side and some marvellous Tiffany cut-outs on the other.

Backstage, the 'Tiffany' screen.

THE GARDEN

I had seen many charming gardens made by dollshouse clubs and Doll House Emporium had a number of items for garden settings. The base is in a cardboard box cut down in front and lined with brick paper to suggest a walled garden. I floored it with large grey card flagstones. The green plastic greenhouse cost only £1, and was found at Miniatura, the plants inside come from a 3D greenhouse card I was sent; the painted "birdhouse" came from a fancy goods shop and acts as a summerhouse. The dovecote was also got at Miniatura as were the tiny plastic doves. I propped mine up on a pencil as it was quite heavy to stick to the wall. The white pillars are from a cake shop as is the cupid topping one, a miniature astrolabe, fashionable in pukka gardens (Sir Roy Strong has one) is on top of the other. The garden seat is the white wire wickerwork as I used in the Corfu Villa. The croquet set is especially charming, and reminds me of croquet games at my cousin Lorna's home. My first flower containers were bought at Tiny Town. made by Pat the owner, from discarded plastic containers covered with wood effect Fablon with oasis and silk flowers. I bought stacks of paper roses from a Card Craft shop and stuck them on the wall, drawing green felt pen lines between them to suggest a climbing rose, and drew in leaves but later discovered exquisite little glass leaves in Paris which I stuck on over them. I also bought a length of perfectly modelled ivy in metal, to trail around one of the pillars. Miniature tools are readily available, and over the years I have added a bird feeder, a wheelbarrow, a tortoise, and the resin pond with inquisitive cats, and most recently some young cousins gave me an enchanting hedgehog. Fake grass floor covering is available from many suppliers but I thought the stuff greengrocers use is more realistic and begged a small piece from a local shop. The doll in a poke bonnet I had already, filled with lavender, and later added the peg doll and the small wooden child.

THE CHURCH

This was bought as a kit at the Spring Miniatura in 2008. You can get grander affairs with a tower, but this is all I had space for and it has been a delightful project.

There are many small ancient churches in Britain, several of which I have visited, including my favourite, Mwnt, near Cardigan. Dixe Wells recently produced a book on *Tiny Churches* in Britain which is fascinating. Mine is whitewashed inside as so many are but I have also given it some mediaeval wall paintings, including the famous Wheel of Fortune which I saw at Rochester Cathedral.

Many East Anglian churches have a heavenly flypast of wooden angels, (as Joyce Grenfell described them), carved on the roof beams and so does St Ives' church in Cornwall, where they had to take the angels down for repairs and photographed them as a group, so I used that postcard to cut out my flying angels. The little kit has a rose window as well as arched ones, but actual windows were not supplied so I had great fun creating my own from glass paint on perspex. I made the pews, altar rails and pulpit, the altar was a block of grey painted wood from one of the Ikea houses, intended as a chimney. I modelled the "brass" lectern in Fimo. I also made the long cushions at the altar rails and the tiniest kneelers imaginable to hang in the pews, terrified constantly of losing them till tacky-waxed in place. Looking at them now I cannot think how I could see to work on such a tiny scale. The font was modelled on a mediaeval one in our church. The chest at the back of the church is a 1/24th scale one and holds small metal prayer books provided by Teepee Crafts.

It was enjoyable finding the dolls to occupy the pews and the pulpit, I dressed the preacher suitably in surplice and gown. I rewigged some of the dolls as they all looked alike or re-painted their hair. As a member of the Mother's Union I made a banner to prop in the corner by the altar.

EASTER ROOM BOX

In *Dolls House World Magazine* in April 2001 was an enchanting project by Veronica Godfrey to make this. I kept a look out for a suitable box and my son Guy gave me this neat, red, wooden one intended for use as a display case.

I liked Veronica's project so much I copied it exactly, making the wall paper like hers and embroidering the cushion and cloth from her pattern. I even managed to find the minute blue and white eggcup just like hers, at Miniatura and modelled a chocolate egg in Fimo to put in it and a simnel cake which also appears on the table. The Easter egg tree, however was an idea in *Dollshouse and Miniature Scene* in March 2002 where they also provided cut out boxes for the Easter eggs and Easter cards. The paper plate, painted to look like a clock and the wall vase were my ideas too, and the yellow canisters on the table and set of tiny fluffy chicks came from Miniatura. We have always especially celebrated Easter, when the children were small they made Easter gardens, and we had a branch hung with wooden Easter eggs as well. Now that they have all flown the nest, I still have the tree and like to stand my cheerful roombox beside it in Easter week.

CHRISTMAS SCENE & CHRISTMAS HOUSE

I have always decorated the sittingroom dollshouses for Christmas and many Christmas things are available in miniature. Part of our fullsize Christmas display since I acquired it in 2005 at Soest's Dollshouse Fair has been the superb cardboard backdrop pictured below.

From a shop display originally, I paid 15 euros for it and love setting it up each year with fake snow, a present from a friend, which is carefully swept up every year and saved for the next. The Christmas tree on the left is moulded beautifully in porcelain, and the sleigh on the right belonged to my mother and was always part of our decorations at home. The Christmas stall came as a kit from Arnhem Dollshouse Fair and cost 12 euros. The lovely green and red holly patterned material decorating its roof and counter, were found at Cardigan Market. It is full of the most exquisite miniatures, most bought at a dollshouse fair in Paris, from Le Coffre Emilie and La Maison de Caroline, but the tiny paper nativity came from Soest. On the counter is one of those miniature South American folk art creches which are readily found in Fair Trade shops. The doll running it is of the type often sold dressed in national costumes and was bought at Soest. She wears a hand-knitted cap and scarf,

CHRISTMAS HOUSE

I had seen several examples of these in various magazines and bought a £19.99 kit at the Old Barn in Aberaeron, to make one myself. I painted it red and white to look like Scandinavian houses. One is often told it is wiser to paint a house before assembling it, not good advice however for these flimsy kits as they tend to warp and then are hard to assemble. However the end result was satisfactory and I had a field day with all the miniature Christmas patterned material found at Cardigan Market - the wonderful haberdashery store downstairs was a source of pleasure and useful items for years. But the red braid edged curtains were a Christmas napkin found in a charity market. The sleigh bed, so appropriate but of course an American name for this style of 19th century bed, is covered with identical material to that used to decorate the Christmas stall, above.

The pretty embroidered binca carpet with poinsiettas in the bedroom was bought at a Christmas Fair in Dolgellau. The washstand has red towels made by me and Santa's striped nightshirt, made from my old pyjamas. The slippers are made from chenille pipe cleaners. Mrs Santa's cape hanging on the wall was a simple pattern in

Dolls House World February 2002. Their Craft Club also provided the resin figures of Santa and Mrs Santa. Santa stands in his office reading a Christmas list. Red binca sacks of toys lie about ready and his desk is covered with letters from children. The desk and chair are part of a painted kit from No 50 in Machynlleth, Mrs Beaumont's wonderful dollshouse shop. Pat in Tinytown made the wool carpet. The carpet in the sittingroom is a table mat, from an old set bought in Spain, I made the brick fireplace hung with stockings, and the armchairs and tuffet covered with gold patterned holly material from Cardigan.

The swags were bought in Soest, originally I made some from railway modelling moss and trimmings but they do not last permanently and are apt to "weep" so have been replaced. I made almost all the food from Fimo, apart from the paper gingerbread men bought at Miniatura, and am especially pleased with the chocolate log and its miniscule robin. I painted the paper plates and made the crackers from Fimo, an idea which I think is original, I have made boxes of them for dollshouse friends for Christmas. The red and white theme continues in the kitchen - I painted a kit counter white with red handles, the red edged bowls were a set found at Miniatura as were the copper items. This too is displayed and lit at Christmas and gives great pleasure. The tiny sleigh out front was found in in a fancy goods shop and contains a sack of reindeer food bought at Miniatura. The pottery dwarf was bought at Arnhem Fair, and I found the reindeer in a model shop, he likes chewing the swags!

COLLECTIBLES

My collectable houses are often rescues so not perfect but it is interesting to have all the examples whatever their condition.

DAS BIEDERMEIER SPIELZEUGHAUS

This wonderful book published in 1987 was found at Monika Schluter's Doll's Hospital and Shop in Jakobi Strasse in Soest. I paid 15 euros for it.

It depicts, as it says, a toyshop of the Biedermeier era and the book itself folds out to form the popup shop and house above it. Biedermeier refers to a style current between 1815-1848 in Austria and Germany but was imitated in other countries too, a simpler style of living than the excesses of the French style of the eighteenth century. On the right is a very neat German park and on the left a vignette from a town like Rothenburg, one of the most beautiful old towns in Germany on what is called the Romantic route in Bavaria.

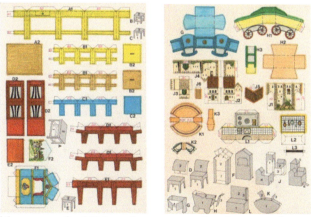

The double page of additional press-out furniture and toys, which I have never set-up as I wanted to keep it in its pristine condition.

MARKS & SPENCER PENNY BAZAAR

This charming little paper model was printed by Parragon Past Times Series in 1993 for £4.99. It is described as an *Edwardian Shop* devised and illustrated by Sue Shields. The book gives a potted history of shopping and of Marks & Spencer.

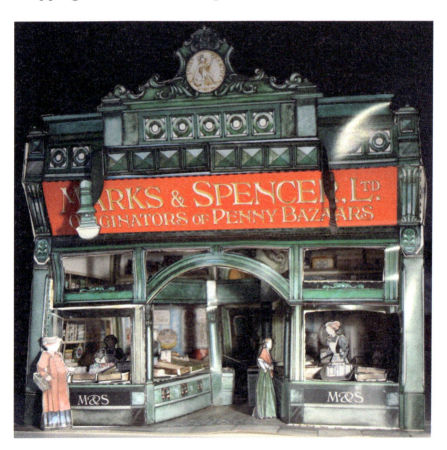

Interior of the Penny Bazaar

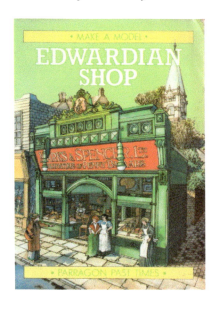

GERMAN BATHROOM

This was bought at Monika Schluter's shop in Soest for 80 euros in 2006. An earlier, more elaborate version circa 1920s, is illustrated in Faith Eaton's *The Ultimate Dollshouse* book.

Mine has a plastic bath and basin instead of a tin one and the electric light above the bath and the taps for the bath had broken, - it can actually fill with water from reservoirs at the back and the basin also. I replaced the taps with sections of bendy straws painted silver. These became as popular toys as the ubiquitous German kitchens and continued to be made until the 1950s. I have added the toilet roll hanger, towel, toothbrushes and toothpaste and mug, all found at Miniatura and the bath tray with its minute plastic duck as well as the vintage white wooden bench.

On the back of the German Bathroom, these two reservoirs allow real water to run into the bath and sink.

GOTTSCHALK HOUSE

Morris Gottschalk was a very well-known German dollshouse maker who operated from 1891 to the 1930s. His houses are very collectible and sell for hundreds of pounds so I never expected to be able to afford one. However, Celia Thomas of Ktminiatures offered this for sale for £90 because part of the facade was missing and the characteristic red roof had been overpainted with black paint although the previous owner had managed to remove some of this. But it had its original wallpapers and curtains and lampshades. It dates from 1924.

I already owned a 1930s German doll and some German furniture as it is generally much cheaper to collect than English furniture of equivalent date and has lots of character. Upstairs is a German tin bath dating perhaps from the 1920s as mentioned above which can fill with water and was bought as it stands in an antique shop in Trier, Germany for 20 euros. They now sell at about £29. All the furniture shown here was bought at Golland's stall at Miniatura apart from the fireplace which was got at a charity stall for £2, at Miniatura. The armchairs are Japanese and also pre-war. Celia kindly sent a photocopy of a catalogue to show how the facade would originally have looked.

My Gottschalk house and below, how it may have looked when new.

Gottschalk house, the tin bath.

Gottschalk house, sitting room.

WAGNER HOUSE

Dollshouses made by the firm of D H Wagner & Son, Grunhainichen, Germany, are also very much sought after and sell for several hundred pounds. They were imported into Britain between 1928 and 1938.

This 24th scale version was bought in a half-price sale from Wendy Allin's stall at Miniatura in October 2009 for £45 complete with much of its Dinky-made furniture. I instantly recognized it as a Wagner house because of its characteristic painted timbering and orange-red stenciled roof, the deep brown-painted base is typical also. These features appear on a Wagner house illustrated in Valerie Jackson Douet's *Dollshouses: A Collector's Guide*.

The metal suites of bathroom and bedroom furniture it contained were made for a Dolly Varden printed cardboard house of the 1930s all made by Dinky toys and were often referred to as Dolly Varden furniture and examples are illustrated in Olivia Bristol and Lesley Geddes-Brown's book: *Dolls Houses*. This furniture often suffers from metal fatigue but even so sets like the ones in this house, sell today for as much as £80. Mine are perfect, apart from a missing drawer in the dressingtable.

The house also contained a yellow metal simulated wicker armchair which retails now at £11. I have since been able to find for £7 a Dolly Varden kitchen table, (market price today £27) and a very battered Dolly Varden kitchen dresser. I added the fireplace in the house, which is by Triang.

The Wagner House and below, Dolly Varden kitchen table and Triang fireplace.

THE YELLOW HOUSE'S FURNITURE

This rather striking house painted yellow hence the name, was bought at auction at Llannarth for £22 by a friend who gave it to me for my 70th birthday. It is obviously home-made, opens front and back which is convenient as the rooms are rather low-ceilinged and deep. Considerable trouble has been taken to create a roof with tile marked strips, and heavy ridges, it was apparently originally painted green as I could observe as two ridges were missing and have been replaced by me. The rather clumsy windows open. There were side openings too for access to two small rooms, I have made these into a bathroom and kitchen. Its scale at more one twelfth than the usual one-sixteenth for dollshouses, has made it possible to furnish the main rooms with larger pieces of furniture from my collection. The brass bed in the main bedroom is modern, the patchwork quilt was found on a little stall with an honesty box alongside on the Isle of Tresco in the Scillies. The dressingtable and wardrobe date from the 1920s, one might have thought they were made by Elgin of Enfield but they are not marked as such. The wardrobe especially has been made with great care and has a shallow carved pattern of a flower on each door, possibly a rose. They are obviously a pair as the wood and drawer and door knobs are identical. The fireplace is a metal one but not like the usual Romside ones, plain pink with a hearth. The chest of drawers is lightly stenciled with lemons, the drawers are false as it opens like a cupboard and may be German. All were acquired from S W Golland's at Miniatura. The small bedroom has a Barton bed, and one of those imported from China dressingtables but this is nicer than usual with yellow-painted drawers. In the sittingroom below is a Romside fire but set in a wooden surround, probably by Barton. The sofa and armchairs are in fretwork and upholstered minimally in velvet. These originated as handiwork for disabled soldiers and date from 1914 into the 1920s. Handicrafts of Kentish Town was one of the workshops, and their products are illustrated in Margaret Towner's seminal book on *Dollshouse Furniture*. There is also a more elaborate fretwork armchair of similar date. All were bought on S W Golland's stall at Miniatura for £30. The blue Art Deco furniture was bought from Ktminiatures in 2010. It is so unusual to find such very Art Deco pieces, I could not resist them, there is also a very well-made solid, brass clock dating perhaps from the early 20th century. The kitchen has a Barton dresser, sink and stove, and the bathroom a Doltoi bath and a 30s metal washstand. I embroidered all the carpets. The occupants are two china dolls, one late 19th century with china head, arms and legs with tiny heeled shoes, very typical of that time, and a mass of hair, dressed as she is now, she cost £25 on

Golland's stall; and the small one with very 1930s marcelled hair painted silver. I paid £11 for her at Golland's and dressed her myself. They are Miss Pettitoes and her niece Valeria.

Y BWTHYN BACH TÔ GWELLT/PRINCESS ELIZABETH'S WELSH COTTAGE

My first encounter with this charming dollshouse was in 1947 when my parents bought one for my sister in the Argyll Arcade, Glasgow. Triang produced this facsimile soon after the cottage playhouse was given to Princess Elizabeth, then aged six, in 1932 by the people of Wales: the words Y Bwthyn Bach Tô Gwellt mean the little thatched cottage.

If you go online and look it up you will see the story

of its rather adventurous delivery by lorry to Windsor Great Park and recollections of the children of people involved in the gift. The cottage is still in situ and has been played with by several generations of children, Princess Beatrice recently showed Andrew Marr round it for a TV programme, but they looked a bit like *Alice in her Adventures in Wonderland* when she inadvertently grew rather than shrank. I went online because I had by then acquired the dollshouse myself and wanted to be sure of furnishing it exactly in the right way. Celia Thomas of Ktminiatures advertised one for sale at £90 rather less than they are actually worth because the original windows had been replaced and the wallpaper was damaged, but within reach of my pocket. I was very pleased to have one at last to add to my collection. Interestingly, it must be earlier than my sister's as the fireplaces in her house were of white wood with realistic flames on a black background, (there is one in the Wagner House). These have tiled and wood surrounds and were advertised by Triang as early as 1921. My house also has the thin dowelling banisters, which were later replaced by a solid block of wood. The only furniture hers contained was a white wooden dresser and sink unit. I had managed to find one of the latter on a charity stall some years ago, it lacks its base. Princess Elizabeth's cottage had a Welsh dresser but otherwise, from what I have seen, the furniture was 30s in style and thanks to Celia again I was able to furnish the bedroom appropriately, with Barton beds, dressingtable and wardrobe and armchairs.

The Barton beds rather unusually slot into a single bedhead. I bought the wooden vintage washbasin and loo from Celia too, and filled the bathroom then with appropriate odds and ends I already had. The Barton table and chairs in the sittingroom were bought from a friend as were the chintz armchair and sofa. She gave me the Barton grandfather clock. The wooden standard lamp carved all of a piece with its shade, was found in a charity shop. There is a Barton "Tudor-style" sideboard. I could not find a proper period dresser so have used one already in my possession, one of those often sold as ornaments -

they are made on the Continent and have painted wooden pots. As it is mainly seen sideways on when you open the house it looks suitably heavy. Celia supplied the fridge and Barton kitchen table and chairs.

The stove is exactly like one in my dollshouse kitchen in the 40s, a metal Crescent cooker. The dolls representing the little Princesses, I already had, one is a 30s German doll with moulded hair and the other a very early plastic doll with very blue eyes like Princess Margaret. The books they are reading are tiny facsimiles of Beatrix Potter's books of which a set came with the original house. Serendipitously when my son inspected the attic, in the farthest corner he found a tiny wooden bowl and a miniature book! Incidentally my house has only one deep opening in the roof, extending to the chimney, while some houses had two smaller ones. My Triang label is a triangle within a circular sticker, alongside the opening. I added a contemporary portrait of the Duchess of York as she was then, (the Queen Mother) over the sittingroom mantlepiece, as in the gift cottage. That was painted by the Welsh portraitist Margaret Lindsay Williams.

STONE COURT: A HANDICRAFT HOUSE 1933

This house was bought sight unseen as the result of an advertisement in a Stroud newspaper taken by my old friend Marita Ward, also a dollshouse fan, who lived there for many years. I telephoned the advertiser Mrs Vanessa Evans, Stone Court, Stone, Gloucestershire, who said she thought it was a 40s house, built to a wartime plan and based on an actual house in Bristol. It was £20 and I paid £12.40 postage.

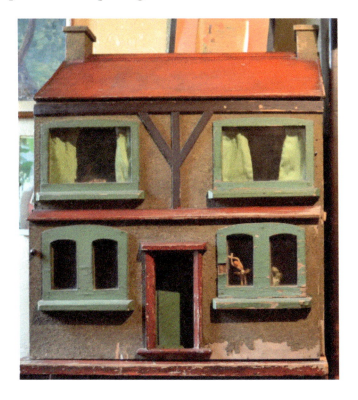

When I sent a photograph to invaluable Marion Osborne, she identified it as made from a Handicraft pattern of 1933. For its age it was in very good condition, a little of the sandpaper on the outer walls was missing, and it needed some new screws for the hinges. The windows are glass. The staircase is given minimal space but care has been taken to create branches to the upstairs rooms. There are no internal doors. There are original wallpapers in all 4 rooms. In three rooms they had been covered over and some attempt had been made to remove the later papers, which, by damping carefully I was able to remove, after photographing the house as it was. I have retained two walls of the later paper in the kitchen as it was lighter than the original. The floors appear to have been veneered in rosewood. There is a tiny back opening in which I have placed a loo. I have not given it a bathroom as many 30s houses did not have them. The children's bedroom cum nursery has a set of Codeg plastic furniture; the bedcover, with its rather overscale pattern of rabbits, is similar to the bedroom curtains in my nursery in 1938, and the charming wooden dollshouse was bought through Hickleton Collector's Club based at Sue Ryder shops. There is a wooden Doltoi fire from Ktminiatures. I made the miniature farm, the animals and gates were supplied at a Railway Modeller's shop. It is an exact copy of the one I had as a child. A favourite Arthur Ransome book is on the bed, a beautifully made facsimile by Celia of Ktminiatures. There is a Doltoi picture on the wall bought at Argylle Arcade, of a mouse house and the other pictures are all 30s themed. One child is a Doltoi doll, with plastic feet, the other a late Grecon type, with wire feet. The sunflower carpet was a pattern from The *Dolls' House Magazine* July 2005.

The very 30s design carpet in the parents' bedroom (not shown) was also made by me from a pattern in *Dollshouse & Miniature Scene* in September 2002. I worked it in tapestry wool rather than embroidery thread which made it more solid but not too bulky for a dollshouse. The parents room' has a rather curious plastic bed, it has a 30s style sunburst at head and foot and though more suitable in size for an adult dollshouse doll actually was originally made as a cradle with rockers, I had one when I was a child, bought at the local newsagent's and fancy goods shop. This one has had its rockers cut off when I found it. The green china washbasin is vintage, and the wardrobe a late Barton with its splayed legs. The nicely made chest of drawers was part of a collection of handmade furniture found by my son Guy in a Cardiff charity shop, together with a similar chest of drawers and the sideboard in the sittingroom, and the kitchen table, chair and corner cupboard.

The armchairs in the sittingroom were bought at Gunter Witt's stall at Soest, he specialised in 30s and 40s furniture. The 30s lamp came from Golland's stall and there is a Barton fireplace bought from Ktminiatures and a Kleeware 40s wireless. I found the flying ducks at Miniatura. In the kitchen the stove is a plastic one, stamped Made in Romania, found in a charity shop, with a Kleeware sink, and Brimtoy tin fridge and an unusual little cast-iron heater also found at Golland's. The wooden teaset is the kind sold in a wooden apple. Mr Stone is a late Doltoi with plastic feet, I am not sure about Mrs Stone with her high-heeled boots. I embroidered the rug by the hearth from Sue Hawkins' Carpets and Rugs, already cited.

Stone Court, the sitting room.

****

EATON & MUNBY's Bungalow 1930s

I bought this delightful little bungalow for £75 from Celia at Ktminiatures, she said she was sorry to part with it. It comes in a neat painted wooden box which provides the base for the house and then a lawn with path leading up to it. The walls slot together and the roof balances on now rather fragile beams which slot on to the walls and the partition which gives 2 small rooms. If you want to see inside you must remove the back wall. It is really more to look at than play with, but I had longed for a bungalow having seen so many delightful 30s ones illustrated. Marion Osborne in her exhaustive book *A-Z 1914-1941 of Dollshouse Makers*, shows a folding dollshouse they made, identical to mine. It retailed in 1934 at 25 shillings. The firm, based at Burley, Ringwood, in Hampshire, seems to have only been active for a few years.

I have turned it into a small museum for my mother's cousin "the most famous Welshwoman of her day", Sarah Jane Rees, better known by her bardic name Cranogwen. Born in 1839, she edited a woman's magazine, regularly preached, won a bardic chair at a National Eisteddfod, and lectured in America. She was born in a cottage very similar to this and the exhibition has a few items of Welsh furniture, miniature photographs and information boards.

Munby bungalow packed into its box.

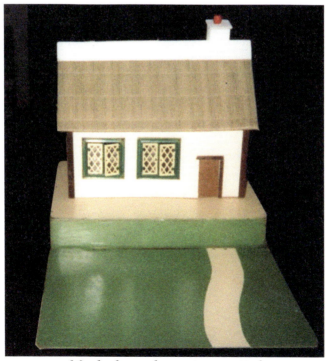

Munby bungalow set up on its base.

THE DWARFS' COTTAGE

This was in my possession before I was born, my mother photographed the nursery she and my father had prepared for me, their first child, and on top of the wardrobe appears the dwarfs' cottage.

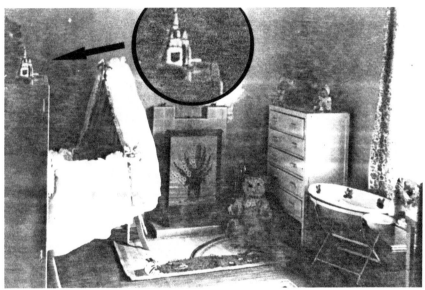

My childhood nursery with, inset, the Dwarf's Cottage.

I was born in October 1938. Scarcely a year before in December 1937, Walt Disney released his animated film *Snow White & the Seven Dwarfs*, which ended up becoming the highest grossing film of all time, its novelty with beautiful colour made it an instant hit and a great deal of merchandise was produced in the wake of its appearance including the cottage.

The original figures of Snow-white and the dwarfs were made of lead which is probably why I don't remember them. They were perhaps removed for safety. But I have always cherished the little house, and it sits in a glass cabinet with 7 dwarfs (Christmas cake decorations).

"Ye Dwarf's Cottage" from the Walt Disney film 'Snow White and the Seven Dwarfs' which I have owned since 1938.

DUTCH WAREHOUSE

This typically Dutch toy was acquired at an antique shop at Zanse Schans in the Netherlands, a Folk Museum similar to St Fagans in Cardiff. I paid the equivalent of £33, but think I was lucky as I have since seen similar ones for sale at fairs at three times the price.

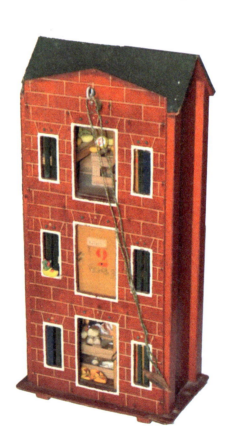

The 'Clog Shop' on the ground floor of the warehouse.

It is difficult to date because they were made over several decades, but probably dates from the 1940s. Some of the window slats were missing and have been replaced, and a child had scribbled on the sliding wooden doors. The hook for the hoist was missing so I have replaced it and added a rope to go round the peg lower right. It was completely empty when I acquired it except for a lot of dust! I have placed slatted tables inside to hold cheeses and clogs and put neat wood labels on the doors saying Kaas and Klompen. I made the cheeses in red and yellow fimo, and glazed them to look waxed. Arnhem Fair provided the clogs: it was worth shopping around there as prices varied from 1 to 2.50 euros.

'Cheese' is stored on the top floor.

TIN HOUSES: LOUIS MARX & CHAD VALLEY

Tin houses are not uncommon in England having been made by Chad Valley and Mettoy some 50 years ago but my first tin house was sent to me in 2000 from the USA by my son Lew who found it in a Goodwill store (like our charity shops) on Long Island. They were sold flat packed but this one was already set up, and he dismantled it to post it, they do warp quite easily over the years, so it can then be quite hard to reassemble them. It is also important to make sure they are completely supported on a solid surface or they can warp again. It took quite a lot of patient work with a light hammer by my elder son to ensure every part of it was straight once more.

They are fun with their cheerfully litho'd exterior and interior decoration. The integral windows were unglazed, and have been glazed with perspex. The best-known maker is of course Louis Marx, and Valerie Jackson Douet in her *Dollshouses: A Collector's Guide* has useful information about him. But the maker of this house is not known. I have furnished it with American 'antiques', being a fan of American Folk Art, there is a fabulous collection in Washington DC which I had seen in 1963 and had also seen Henry Du Pont's beautifully-displayed collection at Winthertur, Delaware, when I was staying with a student friend who happened to be a Du Pont descendant. In fact my Greyhound trip around the States that year was geared quite heavily towards dollshouses, seeing the collection at the Museum of the City of New York, (where I was horrified at how dusty and neglected the dollshouses then were) and Mrs Thorne's Rooms and Colleen Moore's amazing dollshouse in Chicago. I had bought Flora Gill Jacob's fascinating *History of Dollshouses* but regretfully never saw her Museum at Washington DC, not in existence then, which was closed down soon after I was there in 2003 and the collection dispersed. I made the 'colonial' bed with its net canopy and little Red Schoolhouse applique quilt, in the main bedroom, and the Amish chest alongside (I visited Pennsylvania's Amish community) and the Raggedy Anne doll seated on it and the Shaker boxes for storage.

The beautiful stool is made from an antique piece of bead embroidery I inherited. I made the tiny tin sconces too. The children sleep in painted bunk beds in the small bathroom next door (not shown) which has a Kleeware bathroom set and a loo I modelled in Das and painted to match it. The kitchen is modern with a Lundby sink and cabinets unit, and all the food is in American packaging, photocopied and reduced in size from Sunset Magazine.

The diningroom next door has a drinks mat from New Orleans as a carpet and plain Taiwan furniture but I made the antique overhead light and modelled a Thanksgiving dinner in Fimo complete with pumpkin soup in a hollowed out pumpkin.

The livingroom has what is described in American 'Country Living' magazine as a buffalo pattern (ie bright check) homemade sofa and painted cupboard, clock cabinet and table from a set acquired at Eve's in Towyn. I made the armchairs too in red and white check with. Amish designed applique cushions with tulips on them. I made the parents Frank and Betty Carroll from Das, Frank's denim jeans are particularly successful, and all the magazines and newspapers are US in origin, there is even a baseball bat and glove and a minute handful of dollars.

The TV was a magnet found by Lew, and it works briefly if you press the knob, and says Twilight Zone with appropriate music!

On the wall are US items, a wooden merry-go round miniature horse and a tiny enamelled San Francisco Streetcar from a pair of earrings bought there in 1963. The folk art tray on the table was found at a Dollshouse fair in Freeport, Long Island. The children are modern dolls, Audrey, the younger one dates from the 50s and is of moulded plastic. The other one, Sylvie, a well made articulated china doll, has paper dolls to play with: when I was young my American aunts sent us the most gorgeous paper dolls and they were favourite toys.

American tin house, with Lundby cabinets.

LOUIS MARX HOUSE circa 1950-1960

Louis Marx was a well known toy maker who became a millionaire. He was making tin toys on his own account from 1921 including dollshouses and, later on, good quality plastic dollshouse furniture and dollshouse dolls. His firm ceased trading in the 1970s. My house has plastic windows hence the later date. But the tabs, chimney and roof are all tin, though after this date they were made of plastic.

I bought this house on Long Island in Northport antique shop for 75 dollars, complete with its plastic furniture, apart from the yellow plastic bedroom set which was found in Freeport, Long Island, at their dollshouse fair, as was the miniature Chinese scroll. The metal rocking chairs were found at a yard sale in Huntington, Long Island.

The dolls and the car in the garage were bought at Woolworth's: they fitted the scale of the house and its furniture perfectly. I have named them for the Beverley sisters, a popular singing group of my youth: Joy, Teddie and Babs. The china with the American flag was a special offer in a magazine. Again American products appear in the kitchen including a minute tomato ketchup tube and Coca Cola bottles. The sittingroom carpet is one of Pat's from Tinytown and I embroidered the rose patterned one in the right hand bedroom.

The car is very amusing - it extends, and when you press the steering wheel plays a tune! After my experience with the previous house warping when dismantled, I brought this one home in a humidifier box stuffed with my clothes, I was luckily travelling by sea. The suspicious lady Customs officer said to me "Don't you have humidifiers in Britain?" so I said "Yes, but it's a dollshouse, look I have written tin house on top", she went away laughing!

LOUIS MARX BUNGALOW

This delightful little tin bungalow is illustrated in Valerie Jackson Douet's book. Mine was bought on ebay for £15, but turned out the seller Diane White of Bettws Bledrws, was based only a few miles from my home, near Lampeter.

It is furnished with Renwal furniture and a very small Barton flock sofa. When I bought it, it lacked its chimney top but was otherwise in excellent condition.

Louis Marx Bungalow

Louis Marx Bungalow

****

Chad Valley Rose Cottage in its box.

CHAD VALLEY ROSE COTTAGE

This tin house was bought in its original box from Celia at Ktminiatures, with my son Guy's help, who contributed part of the cost as a birthday present. It had previously been owned by Margaret Towner, whose invaluable guide to collecting Dollshouse Furniture I frequently consult. It had never been erected but I wanted to have it on display. The windows are unglazed so I have glazed them with perspex.

As the interior is so colourful I have furnished it quite minimally. In the 1950s and early 1960s when it was made, the furniture would most likely have included Kleeware pieces and I have a Kleeware bookcase in the sitting room, filled with cardboard strips depicting books, there is a Kleeware sink unit in the kitchen,and there is a Kleeware bedside cabinet. The bathroom has a Doltoi bathroom set, the double plastic sink came with the Louis Marx house. The bed is German and the dressingtable, its stool and the little chest of drawers are probably made in Hong Kong. The plastic kitchen stove is Doltoi, the fridge is a Triang Prestcold and retails these days at £15 and is a very nicely made plastic one with an opening

door and shelves. The tables
in the house are slot together card ones, bought as part of a suite of rooms sold by the National Portrait Gallery in 2010, (designed for the Metropolitan Museum of Art in New York), which I do not have on display, so they have found a temporary home here. The sofa and armchairs were a gift from my niece Sami at the time, rather unusual with American cloth seats and gold braid trimming. The inhabitants are modern plastic jointed dolls, known as Ted and Rosa.

Chad Valley Rose Cottage, pre-printed decoration with a Doltoi bathroom set.

AMERSHAM HOUSE 1930s-1940s

I was bowled over at seeing this perfect Amersham House for sale at £80 on the Cancer UK stall at Miniatura in 2010, as the only previous one I'd seen for sale was one for £90 at the Parade, Shrewsbury, which lacked its windows. One of the sure ways of identifying an Amersham house is by its characteristic lattice windows in which the tops are fixed and the lower sections open. These houses were produced in Buckinghamshire from the 1930s to the 1950s so are quite hard to date precisely. These lattice windows were however in use by 1941.

My house has just two rooms and no staircase. Upstairs there is a Twiggs wardrobe and late Barton bedroom set, and a very nice metal bathroom suite got at Pastimes, Westbury Street, Sherborne for £10, only lacking its linen basket and bathmat. There is also a Barton Tudor chest but minus its original lid. Downstairs has an old wooden fireplace with hearth, a Barton TV in a cabinet with opening doors and a Barton clock on top of it, and a Barton sink and metal red and cream stove, and a Twiggs dresser; the easychairs are home-made, the table and chairs are Barton and date from the 1940s, I bought identical ones in the Argyll Arcade in 1947, likewise the cutlery box, which still retains some of its cutlery. The dolls are a celluloid one in the bath, she is known as Sarah Lloyd as my mother as a child on first hearing the word celluloid interpreted it as Sarah Lloyd; downstairs there is a slightly battered early Grecon doll with metal feet and has possibly been redressed as she wears trousers, instead of the usual felt frock.

HENLLAN

This is a popular Welsh name meaning old sacred place, which I have given to this unidentifiable house because it was bought at an auction in Henllan by a friend in 2009. Subsequently she decided it took up too much space and passed it on to me. It has so many characteristics of commercially made houses but Marion Osborne says she knows of no identifiable maker though very kindly sent me pages from a Romside catalogue which shows that these bay windows were available in 1962 and it has typical Romside doors. A window was missing upstairs and one of the garage doors which have been replaced through Ktminiatures
.

The roofs of the main house and the garage are made of overlapping strips of wood. The upstairs floor on the left is slightly warped, it appears to have its original carpet of rather felt like green paper, and the righthand room has a nice lino-like pattern in brown and white, otherwise walls and floors painted cream. Upstairs the fireplaces are rudimentary from shaped pieces of wood but with Romside fireplaces downstairs. The staircase is behind the non--opening centre panel. The timbering on the gable and the greenery painted on either side of the bays show the influence of Triang.

The house is furnished with a Barton hallstand bought in 1947 at Argyll Arcade although the hall is so small it stands alongside the staircase together with a cupboard and shelf above it, probably German, dated 1910 with a transfer print on the doors. The table is similar in style to Barton but sturdier and painted in a much darker colour with 4 small matching chairs with the seats painted in gold paint. The 30s three piece suite, covered with rather than upholstered in cotton, may be home made. There is a moulded china teatable and a Doltoi doll with metal feet. The kitchen has a well made fridge stamped made in China, which opens to show blue plastic drawers, and a wooden table of the style often described as English in dollshouse books, with a single opening drawer. It could be Barton. The glass teapot, cup and saucer and bowl on the table date from the 1940s, I bought them in 1947. There are two Kleeware plastic chairs and a very nicely made wooden Doltoi stove has printed paper hotplates and the name Main transfer-printed on to it. And a

Lundby sink unit with cupboards above and below. These contain appropriate household goods made by Naomi's Miniatures, tiny Silvo, Mansion polish and the like, also a tin of Colman's mustard. A miniature box of Crawford's biscuits is on the table. The bathroom has a green metal bath, basin and loo and a 1930s cupboard with shelves similar to Barton but with rounded bars beneath it and a brass knob. The dressingtable may be home-made. On it is a Chrysnobon toilet set tortoiseshelled by me. The bedroom has an early Barton wardrobe and a Doltoi bedroom set and modern plastic bunk beds and a blue felt 50s chair. The Doltoi boy has metal feet and is playing with a miniature railway set made by Phoenix to paint oneself, which I have in the colours of my Hornby trainset. The tiny tin fender was found at Golland's stall.

MY TRIANGS

From L to R - Triang 60, 61, 1957-58, 50 & 40.

My earliest Triang in date is probably the Princess dollshouse already described; it is often difficult to date houses precisely, even with Marion Osborne's detailed study of *Lines and Triang Houses* to hand, as identical designs continued to be made for so many years from the 1930s to the 1950s. Most of my other Triang houses date from the 50s and 1960s.

TRIANG 60

My first Triang was bought from a charity stall at Miniatura in 2002 for £54 and carried home on the train and bus with great difficulty in a Tesco folding tray, all that was available! Marion shows an almost identical one in her book, as Number 60.

My house has lost its steps, and chimney and then lacked a casement in the downstairs window which I have replaced. It has also lost the centre strut under the bay window upstairs. Before the war these houses had only two struts and after the war always three. But at least it had its characteristic Triang door furniture with what I call a spoon knocker, which is always found on the older houses.

Triang 60 (my first Triang house)

As the house has only two rooms, I chose to glaze the sunroom at the side and give it an easily removable pair of doors; it is furnished with a very small cream plastic kitchen set which came with my Louis Marx tin house. At the time I had acquired some attractive pieces of

Japanese paper at Miniatura so made the rather startling curtains from them. There was a vogue for all things Japanese earlier in the 20th century, for instance Monet was a great fan of Japanese prints, and his house is still full of them. I made the firescreen in the sitting room, it is an exact copy of that in my parents' bedroom. The fireplace is by Doltoi, 30s style too.

The sittingroom's metal sofa and chairs were in vogue in the 1930s, these were being marketed about 1934 under the tradename Holdfast. Marion Osborne had an article depicting them in colour in *Dolls House World* in March 2004. The radio is also made of heavy metal.

Otherwise the furniture is mostly modern Taiwan, I particularly like the green painted set in the bedroom. The tiny green armchair is home-made. I made a screen (pictured on the left of bedroom) to divide the bedroom from the bathroom, which has a Sylvanian, bath a home-made loo and the basin is a "find", as they are invisible anyway. The dolls are a Hobbies set, and I made the Moses basket from embroidery canvas. I also made the 30s carpets and the Art Deco cushion, the latter from a pattern in *Dollshouse & Miniature Scene* in September 2002. The coffee pot and cups were made by Doltoi, but I have painted it in Clarice Cliff style, with washable paint of course!

TRIANG 61

This Triang was spotted from the top of a double-decker bus while on my way to North Wales: I glimpsed its roof sticking out of a cardboard box outside Julian Shelley's shop in Northgate Street, Aberystwyth. I telephoned the shop next day and arranged to come and pick it up as it was only £15.

It proved to be a Triang 61 which I did not have and though the poor thing had suffered terribly as the first photograph shows, with someone having daubed white paint all over it, and being almost windowless, and with some of the brown timbering around the windows missing too, I felt I hadn't wasted my money as amazingly it still had its set of steps which I have since seen offered for sale at £12-£15.

Triang 61 cleaned and with restored windows.

Interestingly it has a grey-blue roof as Marion depicts in her book, unlike the more usual reddish. Careful scraping with fingernails removed a lot of paint from the original really pretty decoration of roses and greenery on either side of the downstairs window, and a lot of paint washed off as well but it was very hard to remove the paint from the roof without obliterating the tiles. It also has just two rooms and the original brownish paper was still in situ. It is certainly postwar as it has three supports beneath the upstairs window not two. I had hoped to replace the windows with Triang ones and narrowly missed a rare set Celia had for sale at Ktminiatures so have had to settle for Romside, which though they make the house look better do not fit as well. They cost £25.

Its occupants are Triang, from their 1960s collection, Jenny of Jenny's Home and her mother, found on a charity stall. Triang began providing furniture for their houses after a long gap in 1960 with ultra modern Spot On Furniture, plastic with metal legs, and by about 1965 this had become Jenny's Home, a series of room boxes with furniture sold to fit together to make a house. According to Margaret Towner these are now very popular with collectors although I can't say I like it as much as earlier pieces. Marion Osborne had an interesting article on Spot On furniture with many coloured illustrations in *Dolls House World* in October 2002.

Upstairs has a Barton four poster bed (not shown) and a Japanese chest of drawers, with a charming painting of

Mount Fuji on its top, over which hangs a mirror I made in 30s style, the other bed is made by Schoenhut and is a set with a bedside table and chair. Margaret Towner writes that Japanese furniture was imported into Britain between 1914 and 1939, most probably between the wars. She recommends it for less well-off collectors! Both were purchased from Ktminiatures. She also says that Albert Schoenhut made hardwood furniture from 1928-1934 in a variety of painted finishes, the bedroom furniture always pink or green, and the furniture rather chunky. The armchairs are home made very nicely, 30s in style and upholstered in pink silk and found like the Schoenhut set at Golland's stall.

Downstairs in Triang 61, note the full size light switches added by a previous owner!

Downstairs there is a Kleeware dresser and sideboard, very well made, as were all their 40s pieces, these were on sale in the Argylle Arcade in Glasgow in 1947 (the year Kleeware began producing the furniture) as was the tiny tray on top of the latter, with a Codeg set of dining table and chairs, a Barton sink and plastic stove. The sun room had no seat when I got it and white paint had irretrievably obliterated any floor covering though the garage had an untouched brick paper floor. The sunbeds are modern plastic and I made the cushions.

TRIANG 1957-58

This was bought for £10 at a Scout Auction in Stroud with some Barton furniture. It lacked its front panel, the garage door and front door and all its windows, that is the frames alone survived; and the upstairs rooms had been decorated, the remainder of the house having their original plain white walls. A room had also been neatly added over the garage, and the original roof retained and carpeted with green grass paper. A doorway has been cut through to the bedroom. Interestingly, a slightly earlier model did have a room over the garage integral with the house. Pam Ruddock wrote about it in an article I already had in *Dolls House World* May 2001. By studying the illustration in Valerie Jackson Douet's book and going carefully through my catalogues, I was able to get the appropriate paper and shutters from Maple Street and the big window from Hobbies, and replace the missing panel, but no one seemed to supply the smaller windows, so I made them, I also made a new up and over garage door and front door, mixing paint carefully to achieve the correct shade of blue.

About this time I found a charming catflap with cat emerging at Thame DollsHouse Fair and could not resist adding it to the door! The additional room held a Barton bath, basin and loo and a Renwal linen basket. Marion Osborne discovered that Kleeware sold moulds to the US company which is why some items are identical. The sitting room has a Barton dining room table and chairs and standard lamp. The sofa and armchair and dresser are

Kleeware. The fireplace is marked Renwal and so is the ashtray stand but lacks its curly plastic handle. There is a Spot On bookcase complete with wooden books. The kitchen set of furniture is made of hard plastic, but the detail is delightful, the fridge has slatted shelves and a nicely moulded door and hinges, and the rest of the furniture made with the same attention to detail.

The small bedroom shown contains Barton furniture but now has a Codeg bedroom suite which looks exactly as if made from caramel. In the main bedroom the pink plastic bed and dressingtable were found at CRAFT. It must be made in Hong Kong or China as has no marks, though the bed with its plastic cover is similar to the Kleeware bed in the opposite corner of the room. The wardrobe and second dressingtable are by Barton. I have put a deckchair and wire table in the "garden" and added a rather nice pet dog. The dolls are Doltoi, the parents have metal feet, the little girl plastic. The house has felt fitted carpets and rather gorgeous fake wool rugs, the material was found at Miniatura.

TRIANG CEX

Marion Osborne decribed this as *"basically the 1930 version in a new dress"*, it does look rather more austere than the earlier versions with their rather cottagey colour and decorated walls. She sent me a page from a catalogue dated 1959 showing the house.

It came complete with its original rather odd oversized glass lights tho they have been damaged probably by using a too powerful bulb. I bought it from Anne Brown at Pastimes Glasgow for £75 and furnished much of it very reasonably from there as well with contemporary or earlier furniture: the red wooden "Vintage " suite in the sittingroom has black American cloth seats so may well date from the 1930s. The table is German. The radiogram is by Barton, (from 1947) as a child I was charmed by its not very realistic wire arm and red turntable. There is a Kleeware television (not shown).

The kitchen is furnished with Brimtoy made from 1951, according to Marion Osborne. I especially like this tin furniture and collect pieces whenever I can, though curiously the rather undersized chairs and table are made of plastic and were added about 1955. The firm ceased trading by 1960.

The bathroom has soft plastic pink furniture; rather amusingly it comes with plastic plugs on chains for its bath and basin. Its colourful "rag" rug was knitted in some unusual wool. The main bedroom has a complete set of Jenny's Home Spot On furniture produced by Triang in the 60s, bought for £16 at Tavistock Market: I was lucky, as the bed alone sells for that sum these days. There is also a Barton cot. The dolls are by Doltoi.

Triang CEX

TRIANG 50

This tin-fronted house has an opening not a sliding front. Marion Osborne's guide shows these houses appearing in the 1950s - the larger ones, ie those with 4 panes up in the windows being earlier than the 3 paned ones, see next house. My niece found me this at CRAFT the Sally Army secondhand store, like the store often did, the staff appear to have over painted the front perhaps because it had rusted, inevitable sometimes with tin, and have stuck two decorative plaques on the house, the original would have had just one, a sundial. But otherwise it is in excellent condition, even with two little trees by the door. These houses were made with no ceiling above the bedrooms only the card roof, which makes it different from the similar tin fronted Triang described below. She paid £25 and kindly gave it to me for Christmas. The windows were unglazed and I have glazed them.

The house originally had four rooms but a previous owner had inserted a partition to make a landing with a curtained door. There was also a small cupboard, and downstairs a false wall had been inserted to create a fireplace and shelves, very nicely done, and a banquette. The bathroom suite by Barton was stuck in place and so were the kitchen fitments linked by shelves to give a fitted effect: a plastic Barton stove and washing machine and a Lundby sink unit. In the sitting room I have added the 30s sofa and armchairs and table bought on Golland's stall and placed a set of shelves on the landing. The bed is by Barton. The pictures already in the house are, I think, Sylvanian. I made the doll, Cristyn, from a porcelain kit.

TRIANG 40

I first saw one of these tin-fronted houses with the laburnum tree decal in an antique shop for £70. According to Marion these, with sliding fronts, were introduced as early as 1950-51 but with slightly larger scale of four panes up in each window (like the previous house) not 3, as in the one I possess. The decals too were different on the earlier house, the laburnum seems to belong to the 1960s.

Mine was found for £2 by my son Lew in a Car Boot Sale, it had unfortunately lost its roof but that was not such a disaster because unlike the similar front opening houses which lacked a solid wood base for their roofs this, as you can see, possesses one. One would have liked to know if the original roof was card or plastic but probably the latter. The windows were unglazed and to dustproof the house I have glazed them. The door was also missing so I have replaced it. The house had only two rooms and no staircase, I inserted a partition to make a bathroom. This is such a cheerful light house I have furnished it accordingly; the bedroom has a Barton suite and a marvellous Renwal treadle sewing machine which Lew found for me on the internet. The small lamp there is Renwal too. The bath is Doltoi and the blue basin similar to that in the pink set in the previous house. The kitchen furniture was made in Czechoslovakia in the 1970s and found on the internet. The ironing board and the coffee table are by Renwal and the fireplace is by Louis Marx bought from Ktminiatures. The sofa is the only recent item and the abstract paintings I put up.

SHERBORNE

This house, although so similar to the Triangs, is not apparently one of theirs. Marion Osborne was intrigued by it never having seen, as she said, one with windows in its sides, and the Lutyens style porch is an attractive feature too. I found it in a railway modelling shop in Sherborne where it was being sold along with some Barton furniture on behalf of a customer. I paid £15, which was a bargain as it was in such good condition.

The wallpaper is not original but can definitely be dated to the 1950s. I bought a lot of the furniture too. The bedroom furniture is all by Barton, and so is the fireplace and armchairs and sofa and a lovely little Barton bureau in the corner; the plastic stove probably is and the sink unit although it has a silver painted double drainer and not the usual white sink and draining board but has sliding doors. The blue table and chairs are by Kleeware. The dolls are Doltoi grandparent dolls bought at Ktminiatures, she has metal shoes but Grandpa has plastic shoes. The charming miniature china lions on the fireplace were found at Miniatura, my parents owned a pair, full size.

Sherborne interior.

MY GEEBEES HOUSES

GeeBee was a trademark of the Tudor Toy Company based in Hull, as Marion Osborne informed me when I sent her a photograph of my first GeeBee house which my son Guy bought for me at the PDSA Charity shop in Penarth for £24.99 in 2004. Tudor Toy first advertised dollshouses in 1949 and made a variety of styles, but with identifiable characteristics, through to their closure in 1978 although the houses continued to be sold by Humbrol until 1981. It had been entirely covered with brick paper, when this was removed the characteristic

GeeBee greenery was revealed on the lower half of the house but not on the upper half of the facade which seems to have been replaced at some time with the addition of a strip of wood which gave it a slight overhang, rather appropriate for a slightly Tudor style house.

I was intrigued by the Hobbit-style doorway: the door itself was missing an so were a couple of casements. The base seems to have been overpainted a paler green than the original and the wood shape above the door repainted to match. There was a slit above the down stairs window. The copy of her article on the houses which Marion sent me explained that it would have held a tin sunblind, a feature introduced in 1953 but because they were unsecured they were easily lost. It also would have had tin shutters on either side of the upstairs windows. One can date the house a bit more narrowly to between 1953 and 1966 as in that year the colours of the windows changed from green and cream to blue and white and Marion who has seen a number of these houses dates mine to 1957-58. The house has three rooms which were just painted white throughout, and a metal staircase and opens to left and right on hinges which Marion says is characteristic of the earlier houses. I replaced the missing casements, through Ktminiatures, and made a copy of the missing door from a photograph of a similar house offered for sale by Pastimes, Glasgow in perfect condition for £40. And was fortunate to be able to buy two pairs of tin shutters three years later on the internet. I also made a cardboard reproduction of the missing sunblind. I have carpeted the stairs, and added banisters at the top of the stairs and furnished the house mainly in Kleeware though the Barton sideboard came with the house and on it is a Barton plaster vase with plastic flowers. There is a Lundby sink unit in the kitchen, and a Renwal vacuum cleaner, but the rest is Kleeware. I added the Romside fireplaces. The inhabitants are Woolworth's dolls, very nicely made, these were sold with a wardrobe of plastic clothes. The adorable babies were found at Miniatura as was the wirework pram.

Sitting room of my first GBs house, with the kitchen shown below

My second GeeBee's house was found on a stall at the Vintage Rally held annually near Aberaeron. I had gone to see the vehicles and had not anticipated there would be stalls, but when I saw this little house for sale at £7 I could not resist it though you do feel rather conspicuous waiting by the side of the road for the bus home with a dollshouse at your feet!

Luckily they are very light houses, being made of hardboard. This has two sliding fronts though the small one on the left was missing, but fortunately it retained one of its blue tin shutters, and I was able to make one to match. This house is clearly post 1966 as it has blue and white metal windows. The little "balcony" was missing: there was a slot in which a piece of card slid in, which I have replaced, as my next house, having the balcony secured, had retained it. The crazy paving paper on part of the base was slightly damaged but I was able to make a piece to match, and also made a sunblind although in fact the front will not slide open easily with the sunblind in place. I have left the metal staircase as it was, painted green. Downstairs is furnished in Kleeeware and upstairs has Barton furniture. The nicely made plastic articulated doll was found at Soest Dollshouse Fair. I embroidered the sittingroom carpet from a design in Sue Hawkins: Dollshouse Do-it-yourself Projects: Carpets and Rugs.

The third GeeBee's house was bought from Pastimes in Glasgow in 2005 for £65. These double gabled houses were available from 1949, and this has still the green and cream metal windows, and their characteristic shutters and sunblinds though the former are made of wood not tin, and I am lucky to have found a house where the sunblinds have survived.

With all the care taken to decorate the exterior, it is surprising to find such a mingy little doorway and not even a proper door but simply a window. As Marion said apropos of the bare interiors too it is as if they ran out of steam! It doesn't even have a staircase or internal doors. I have laid appropriate paper on the floors. It came with large transfers stuck on the gables by some child and the central chimney was missing, and paper had been stuck on the porch roof with very hard glue. Water had no effect on the transfers but nail varnish remover applied cautiously did the trick tho a slight shadow remains where the transfers have been, and it also removed the glued paper on the porch roof, certainly an improvement. The centre panel is fixed and the two opening fronts are hinged. The bathroom has a Barton bathrooom suite, the most complete I possess, with bathmat and towelrail, often missing; bought from Ktminiatures. The bedroom suite is Barton, from Pastimes, and cost £20.

The kitchen has an eclectic mix of pieces, a Doltoi fridge, a made-in-China but rather nice plastic stove, and two slightly oversize plastic chairs found at Golland's, the wooden table is German and holds a Barton plastic coffee set, and the dresser is by Lundby. there is an unusual but sadly incomplete washing machine by Renwal. The sittingroom has a Barton Tudor table and two Barton Tudor chairs and Tudor chest. There is a Barton sideboard and radio, and a Twiggs grandfather clock but its face had to be restored. The fireplace is Doltoi from Pastimes and the yellow velvet sofa and armchairs are Lundby's "Antique" suite. The dolls are later Doltoi from Pastimes.

The fourth house (above) was found at Pennyfarthing in North Berwick, a bookshop which sells some antique toys. I paid £45 for it with its contents, which included a Barton fireplace alone worth £11.50. Similar GeeBees houses were seen soon after for sale at the Georgian House in Cardigan priced at £75 each. Since they are normally plain white inside it must have been a previous owner who put up the delightful wallpapers. There are no internal doors only rather crude arched doorways. It has the usual metal staircase. Its ridiculously tiny front door was missing, and has been replaced. Above it is the "wrought iron" balcony, this one is fixed. And it still has its tin sunblinds.

Its front opens on dowels rather than hinges, a development Marion Osborne has mentioned in her article and the blue staircase is metal. As can be seen most of the furniture in the bedroom is Barton, the green armchairs and coffee table were available from 1947, there is a Japanese dressingtable and Barton wardrobe, both beds are Barton and one has the little triangular shelf with opening bedside cabinet below. The bathroom has a Barton bath and a vintage china loo and basin, and a German dressingtable. The bed is a plastic one from

Hong Kong but made in imitation of Kleeware. And a Brimtoy dresser and broom cupboard in the kitchen but the latter has a restored door. The stove which has lost its paper hotplates, and fridge and kitchen table and chairs are Barton, the sink is Doltoi. The sitting room has an old sofa bed upholstered by me, and an early Barton TV and fireplace. Alongside that is a Doltoi bookcase with all its original books. The metal standard lamp complete with flex may be by Barrett, it has a plastic shade. A Barrett telephone which has lost its dial, stands on the Doltoi chest. The table and upholstered chairs are German and the coffee set in metal and two small white chairs are Doltoi. It is occupied by a Doltoi family, Mr & Mrs North and their children, Jim and Stella, later models with plastic feet, and their spaniel. I embroidered the sitting room carpet from *Dolls House Projects Winter 2006*, published by *Dollshouse & Miniature Scene*.

My fifth GeeBee house deliberately was not shown in the group photograph because it is so very different from the other 4 but it has a GeeBee label. Marion too had mentioned the open backed Swiss chalet type houses produced in the 70s by Tudor Toy. It is, in my eyes, a very gaudy house and certainly lacks the charm of the earlier houses, but I felt I should buy it to show the range that existed, and it was only £25 in mint condition at the Parade, Shrewsbury.

There are slight similarities linking it to earlier creations: the cladding paper used on the gable is similar to that used on my GeeBees 1 and 2 and the doors continue to be impossibly small, just as with GeeBees three and four. The floors have bright printed carpets though the walls are plain. Having recently acquired some tiny pingpong bats and a ball at Miniatura, I made a ping pong table for the house: we had always had one at home and played it constantly. The bookcases in that room are by Kleeware. The sitting room cum kitchen has a red plastic sofa and armchair by Airfix (1940s) and a Barton kitchen set got from Pastimes for £12.50, dresser, sink unit, table and chairs. The bedroom furniture is mostly German and Czech, and there is a Lundby bed in the right hand room. The dolls are German. A Renwal mangle stands by the outside staircase, and a red plastic laundry basket found at Miniatura.

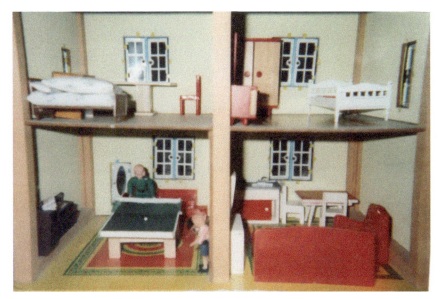

SYLVANIAN WINDMILL

Valerie Jackson Douet includes this in her *Dollshouses: The Collector's Guide*. The Sylvanian families made their first appearance in 1987, charming animals rather than people and were voted Toy of the Year three years running. The windmill appeared in 1990 and Tomy, who make them, have produced many smaller dwellings with very well made furniture and accessories.

My Sylvanian Windmill and Canal Boat.

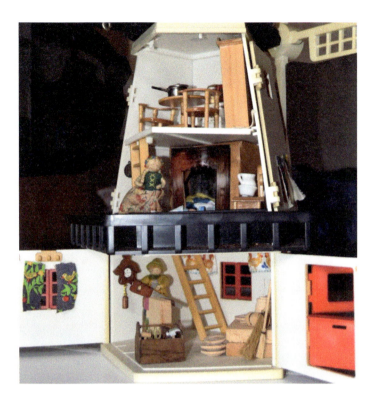

I bought my windmill in the Toy Cave in Aberystwyth in 1999 for £39. I have made mine into a home for two rather special dolls, original Grecon peasant dolls I have owned since I was a child. He is a woodworker by trade, not a miller, as old mills are often re-purposed, and the ground floor has his wood supplies and a number of turned items like whitewood bowls. Their living quarters are on the next two floors. I made the box bed - photocopying the facade, and painted the cradle, and the rest of the furniture is small scale pokerwork pieces I had picked up over the years, made in Taiwan and sold in the Price is Right, Barmouth. The hearth is perhaps an anachronism in this setting but being copper it seemed to fit, these were once sold as ashtrays and are often found in charity shops.

The pretty folk-art curtains have a long history: I used to work sometimes in a shop in summers, and one day a lady came in wearing a dress made from this material, I admired it very much and thought it would make a pretty frock for my daughter, so asked her where she had the material, she kindly said she had some to spare and sent me a length, and these are the left-over scraps!

As the mill came with the characteristic Sylvanian washing line with cloth and tiny pegs I added a wooden washtub and small mangle on the top. I wish I had the original box but in fact I bought the last windmill they had, and it had no box.

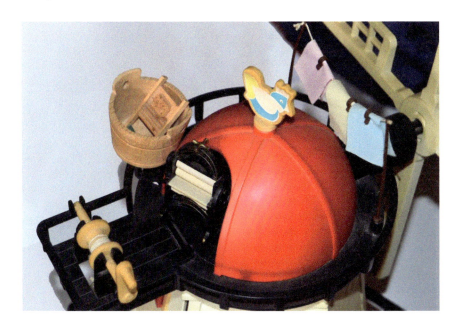

SYLVANIAN CANAL BOAT

This was a birthday present from my son Guy in 2003 and was a big thrill. Although fully-fitted with great attention to detail, there was scope to personalise it with the coloured stickers provided, with floral designs. I also added bedding and lots of decorated china plates, some given by my niece Sami, though the ribbon threaded plate was found at Falkirk Dollshouse Fair. I spent quite a lot of time researching canal boat folk to make sure they were dressed appropriately, Shire Books have an informative publication, and made the clothes myself, the trickiest being the characteristic bonnet worn by canal boat women in the past.

The chap is an anonymous jointed plastic doll found in a charity shop and he has the flat cap and red neckerchief tucked into his waistcoat. His wife is a porcelain doll bought on a Romanian stall at Soest Dollshouse fair and the children are nicely made china dolls available at the Toy Cave or £3 each, and they have a dog. I have made sure to keep the original box in good condition, as all watchers of *Antiques Roadshow* know "Mint & Boxed" are important where antique toys are concerned.

PETITE PROPERTIES' COWSLIP COTTAGE

I am sure Petite Properties' beautifully made houses, works of art in themselves, will be collectors' items in future. They are made of moulded clay on wood and have so much character, especially as in the case of Cowslip Cottage, when artfully distressed. They describe their work as architecture in miniature and stress they are one-off pieces.

They are based at North Scarle, Lincoln. I dithered a long time over their stall at Miniatura because at £64 it was a lot of money for me to spend, normally reserved for purchases of antique houses and vintage furniture. But it was irresistible, and in fact since I bought it their prices have risen considerably.

It is just one up one down, but I created a tromp l'oeil effect of a staircase by making a square shape from card in the corner of the livingroom with a door to suggest a staircase lay behind it and by making a fake door for the bedroom too. The bedroom is furnished with a 24th scale set of pre-war wooden German furniture, bought at S W Golland's stall at the same fair in September 2006 for £7, and have recently seen an identical set for sale at £29 but with the addition of an armchair.

The furniture in the sittingroom is more of a mixed bag, I made the armchairs, the plastic cupboard very nicely made with paper books behind its pretend glassed in top, and the plastic fireplace were found at Golland's, the wooden table and towel rail are from Penny's Toys which specialise in small scale whitewood furniture, at Miniatura too, and the dresser at the back with its display of painted wooden items was found at Soest Dolls House fair as was the miniature wooden Dutch doll made in traditional fashion, jointed like our full size Dutch dolls were years ago. I made her clothes, and also the framed texts in the bedroom (we had loads at home, after our Victorian ancestors who were very fond of them and worked many in cross stitch). She even has some miniscule knitting, found at Soest. I have named her Mrs Sharples after a north-country girl with whom I was at school. Miniature items on the wall include a calendar. In case you are wondering where the stove is, she cooks over the open fire, as I have done myself in the past during the Winter of Discontent in the 1970s, but soot always got into the porridge.

Cowslip Cottage

MOMA

This set of rooms was bought at the National Portrait Gallery in London in 2010, made originally for the Metropolitan Museum of Art by Chronicle books, San Francisco. It has 6 reversible box walls, 8 pieces of press-out furniture which slots together, 6 flooring options, and 13 removable vinyl cling design details.

VERY SMALL SCALE HOUSES

BETSY ROSS HOUSE

In the June-July Issue 1999 *International Dollshouse News* showed The Betsy Ross House - part of the Golden Heritage Series 002. This was the second of two houses created by Hallmark as paper cut-out kits for the United States Bicentennial celebrations in 1976. The other house is simply called the Bicentennial house and shows a pretty eighteenth century interior. Betsy Ross of Philadelphia is famous as the first maker of the American flag, The Stars & Stripes. I immediately thought what fun to own one of the houses but they are hard to find and expensive when found. So I decided to make my own version. I photocopied the exterior of the Betsy Ross house and stuck it on the lid of a wooden box I already had, having covered it first with brick paper. When it came to photocopying the interior, I preferred the design of the Bicentennial House interior so copied that for the inside of the lid, and drew part of the design myself in the interior of the rest of the box. Given the very small scale in which I was working I had to simplify furnishings, I made the four poster bed and the tiny chest of drawers comes from a set of Chinese plastic furniture assembled on a card under the trade name Unicorn, sold by Chrysnobon, and I always bought several at a time, because they were so useful for small scale interiors, they began at about 75p a card but rose gradually to £1.75. The table in the sittingroom is a small plastic Chinese piece and the tray was bought at Miniatura.

Betsy Ross house.

Betsy sits on a matching chair, she was bought at Soest Dollshouse fair and I dressed her myself in a piece of American material, found when my younger son was scrapping some of his (very good quality!) underwear, and if you look closely at the view of Betsy in the window you can see the pattern is almost identical; and made the flag from silk, drawing the design on in felt pen. I am particularly pleased with the view from the window behind her and it is fun to have my own bicentennial souvenir.

MALAMUTE SALOON

I spotted this tiny wooden Bar in a junk shop and instantly envisaged it as the perfect setting for the poem *The Shooting of Dan McGrew* which my mother frequently recited at wartime concerts, she could really make your flesh creep. The poem comes from Robert Service's *"Songs of a Sourdough"* about the Wild West. The furniture of the bar is from the one forty-eighth scale furniture made in China, described above, and I modelled the figures in Fimo. Dan is seated in the corner at the back with *"the lady that's known as Lou"* standing beside him and the mysterious stranger at the piano. There is real sawdust on the floor!

Malamute Saloon, the setting for "The Shooting of Dan McGrew"

Interior of the Malamute Saloon.

FIRST WORLD WAR HOSPITAL

Dolls' House magazine in August 2002 featured a gorgeous collection belonging to Irene Campbell and I particularly liked a World War I hospital called Hoverton Hall after a real house in Norfolk used as a hospital during the first World War. Hers was also only a two roomed building showing patients upstairs in a hospital ward, and downstairs a recreation room for the soldiers with a nurse making tea. The hospital had been made from a meat crate. Having a nice solid little box with a sliding lid made in two halves, I decided to copy it on the same principle as the Betsy Ross house.

I copied the interior carefully, and had space for two beds and a nurse, all of which I had to make, including the Fimo patients in the beds. There is a portrait of Lord Kitchener on the wall just as in the original. I had to make most of the recreation room furniture, apart from the stove and lights which come from one of those miniature sets mentioned above. I decided to add a couple of men in their blue fatigues, which was regulation wear for wounded soldiers. We have a photo of my Uncle Owie in his when invalided out of the medical corps with malaria after serving in Macedonia. This is not my only WWI memorial: for an exhibition we held in our village to mark the centenary of the war, I made a miniature dugout (complete with rat) to a design by Celia Thomas of Ktminiatures, who makes such creations in regular workshops, and it ended up being exhibited at the Welsh Parliament when they borrowed some items for their centenary exhibition.

CHARLES RENNIE MACKINTOSH TEAROOM

My son Guy brought this charming tiny tea-chest to me one day, and said "Can you make something in this?". Obviously it had to be a tearoom and the most famous I knew were the Willow Tearooms designed by Charles Rennie Mackintosh. However it is not an exact copy of the Tea Rooms in Glasgow but rather inspired by his style: I made the tiny furniture from card and the background is mirror card and strips of some plastic netting plus cutouts from Dollshouse magazines.

The miniature tea-chest, which is about 2inches tall.

In which I made a Charles Rennie Mackintosh inspired tea-room.

A MINIATURE PARK

One can work in an even tinier one hundred and forty-fourth scale and I saw these tiny metal figures and park benches and railings at Soest Dollshouse Fair so was tempted to create my own tiny park using a photograph of the famous Carreg Bica rock at Llangrannog as a background.

DOLL'S HOUSE DOLLSHOUSE

Some of my dollshouse nurseries have a dollshouse but not all have been furnished in the detail I attempted here. The furniture is made in cast metal by Teepee crafts, and the tiny dolls were found in Paris where they are displayed tackywaxed to pencils in pots so they don't get lost. I have even made tiny lace curtains for the windows! The actual house is about two inches high.

A RESTORATION PROJECT: THE CARDIGAN CASTLE DOLLSHOUSE

In the spring of 2005 I was taken on a tour of Castle Green house, completely derelict, which had been built within the walls of mediaeval Cardigan Castle. The last family to have owned the house and castle were the Woods and in 1999 Miss Barbara Wood, who had been reduced to living in a caravan in the grounds, moved to a care home. The Castle and house were bought by the Council after local pressure to save it, and to raise funds for the major project of restoring it they allowed guided tours - in hard hats. I must have been the only person in our group who took any interest in the battered dollshouse amid the rubbish inside:

It was obviously insignificant compared to the major problems of torn-up floors (for firewood) and leaking ceilings, but I could not get it out of my mind, I knew it was an unusual house and felt I must make an effort to save it. I thought I had acquired sufficient knowledge to restore it and so offered to do so at my own expense, just one more of the many volunteers already working for the castle. It took months before I heard anything, but eventually the house was delivered to my home in September 2005.

Close to, it was a daunting prospect, the council said it been in a storage depot drying out and had been treated for woodworm but it was thick with cobwebs and dust and in a worse state of disintegration than when I had seen it at Castle Green. In fact at first I could hardly bring myself to touch it or bring it further into the house than the hall, but gradually cleaned it up and as you can see my old cat felt quite at home with it.

It lacked its roof and base which presumably were among the heap of loose timber which came with it; with my son Guy's help we removed it to the garden shed and on a worktable there began putting the jigsaw together again. But I knew it was worth fighting for because of the litho'd gables which had first drawn my attention and which suggested a house of German origin:

That apart, one would have dismissed it as a fairly crudely made home-made house with no access to the roof space and no provision for stairs and no internal doors. The roof was red though this was wholly obscured by an almost immoveable layer of dust. Despite its size, 29" to the roof ridge and "26" by 22" it had only five rooms and was accessible on both sides with four hinged panels, two of which were unfortunately missing. The windows had originally been of real glass, a piece was found in the house, held in place by nails long rusted away and white tape. Providentially one of its original shutters had survived in the house, of printed paper on card. All the upstairs windows had had shutters, some of the downstairs windows had had frames but they had gone, indicated only by their outlines on the facade. Puzzlingly no litho decoration survived on the ground floor except on the surviving side panel. Also missing were pieces of trimming on the exterior indicated by bare patches. The front door had gone, but a shadow on the facade suggested there had been a roof over the door and its adjacent window and I found among the wood, the panel which fitted there, probably supported on posts to make a kind of porch. The internal wallpapers were also of proper dollshouse weight and were beautiful though badly damaged. The only exception were the bathroom and kitchen which looked as if they had been lined with the kind of shelf paper around when I was young (in the 1930s), which was very frail. The floor papers would have survived better if only the appallingly heavy damp and mouldy pieces of full size carpet had been removed, as it was, they had rotted away. Luckily the printed paper pelmets had survived, matching some of the borders on the wallpaper. What remained of the curtains appeared to have been fine black stripes on white and looked like shirt material. It was possibly furnished mostly with home-made furniture: the loo, still in position, was the lower oval of a small tin box stuck to a circular pedestal, and also found in the house was a cloth covered powder box, top rotted, which had once held Oatine face powder. Pathetically all that remained of any dolls were two china legs, one with a heeled boot, and one from a seated doll.

Obviously identification was of the first importance, I consulted all my dollshouse books but there was nothing quite like this, I sent photographs to Marion Osborne and then to the Victoria & Albert Museum but no one had seen a house like this before. Lithographed decoration was used on late 19th and early 20th century German and American houses, but that was the closest I could get to any attribution. A picture stuck on the wallpaper in an upstairs room proved to be a Wills cigarette card of English period costume, these were issued in 1927 and 1929, two such series were listed on the net but not shown so I cannot be more precise. But it suggests that the house was decorated as it stands before 1930.

Providentially the floor papers when installed had been allowed to run up the walls a little way before being covered by the wall papers, and it was these surviving scraps, painstakingly photocopied by Guy until he had once more built up the floor covering, using the repeat pattern, that enabled us to restore the floors to their original appearance or close to it. The same was done with the wallpaper which had survived better, a good section was photocopied to cover the damaged section. I would never have achieved such a thorough restoration without his patient and skilled help, in what time he could spare from his fulltime job as a TV Director. He came up once a month or so from Cardiff with each carefully recreated piece.

Luckily it was fairly straightforward to restore the base and roof, the former had a gap on one side where steps would have been. It was very solid, about 2" deep and measured 31" by 33". I made new opening side panels to replace those lost. And I copied the surviving shutter to create the 15 more required. I also, after some hesitation, made small decorated clay plaques, inspired by wood trim on houses of the period, to fill in the bare spaces under the eaves.

I restored the porch to its original position with sturdy supports and added the panels covered with photocopies of a similar porch on a Bliss house since marks on the base suggested something similar had once been in place there:

Cardigan House following restoration.

I furnished the house as it might have appeared around 1900. It had to be done obviously inexpensively, I spent about £60 on the house, paint, photocopying, and materials. The upstairs drawingroom has reproduction furniture and I made the sofa and armchairs and the centrement which is what this is called in the article showing how to make it by Joan Key in *Dolls House World* in October 2000. The doll seated on it has an unusual blond Victorian china head, I made her on the usual principle of Victorian dolls with stuffed body and china arms and legs, giving her a delightful pair of porcelain shoes found in an antique shop. Appropriately for a locally owned dollshouse she is dressed in Welsh flannel.

Cardigan House, upstairs drawing room.

Dining room (below the drawing room).

The kitchen with the cook: another Victorian china head, I made a body and dressed her. I also made the sink and the tables. The kitchen wallpaper was recreated by hand and the floor is covered with a facsimile of that used in Harrod's Food Hall in 1903.

Upstairs the bedroom is furnished with simple, solid Plan furniture which suits the large room.

The bathroom wall paper again recreated by hand and the floor paper a photocopy of the original as in the other rooms. The bathroom suite was found at a car boot sale for 50p and the towel rail came from Dolls House Emporium.

It was returned to a restored Castle Green house with a full report of the restoration work.

* * * * * *

Collecting and making miniature items has been a huge pleasure over the years and given pleasure to others too who have enjoyed them and not just children. The Welsh Antiques Television programme *Twrio!* sent a crew to make a film of the collection about 18 years ago and even the cameraman was bowled over. (I have added many items since then.) And I have given many talks to groups up and down Ceredigion with smaller items from the collection. Collecting has perforce slowed down in recent years owing to lack of space: there are even 9 houses in the bathroom! You can soap while looking into a Fisher-Price castle and treehouse. Also as I have become more crippled with arthritis, it has become too difficult to travel to the fairs that gave me so much pleasure for many years. The full total is over 140 furnished projects from twelfth to 144th scale. I have made catalogues with photographs of my collection, which now run to five bulky volumes, and decided to use the many lonely weeks of lockdown to write a book about it, a change from writing the histories which have also filled my time for many years. But it too is a form of historical record, when Vivien Greene was writing her book on 18th and 19th century dollshouses, she sought out details of shops and makers, as Marion Osborne has done in her massively-researched books, so wherever possible I too have tried to give details of purchases and makers to assist future dollshouse historians. Incidentally, I also possess miniature versions of several of my publications thanks to the incredible skill of my cousin Ceri's fiancée Elsa! As always huge thanks go to my elder son Guy for his wonderful photographs and to lulu publishing for the opportunity to bring the collection to the wider world. The dedication is to the three friends made since I began collecting and who have helped me so much. Any errors are mine and I apologise for any possibly mistaken attributions, which fortunately in these days of digital printing can be speedily corrected.